RENAISSANCE

VOLUME 10

Technology — Zwingli

GROLIER
EDUCATIONAL

Published by Grolier Educational
Sherman Turnpike
Danbury, Connecticut 06816

© 2002 Brown Partworks Limited

Set ISBN 0-7172-5673-1
Volume 10 ISBN 0-7172-5672-3

Library of Congress Cataloging-in-Publication Data
Renaissance.
    p. cm.
Summary: Chronicles the cultural and artistic flowering
known as the Renaissance that flourished in Europe and
in other parts of the world from approximately 1375 to
1575 A.D.
Includes index.
Contents: v. 1. Africa–Bologna — v. 2. Books and libraries–
Constantinople — v. 3. Copernicus–Exploration — v. 4.
Eyck–Government — v. 5. Guilds and crafts–Landscape
painting — v. 6. Language–Merchants — v. 7. Michelangelo–
Palaces and villas — v. 8. Palestrina–Reformation — v. 9.
Religious dissent–Tapestry — v. 10. Technology–Zwingli.
    ISBN 0-7172-5673-1 (set : alk. paper)
    1. Renaissance—Juvenile literature. [1. Renaissance.]
    I. Grolier Educational (Firm)
    CB361 .R367 2002
    940.2'1—dc21
                                          2002002477

For information address the publisher:
Grolier Educational, Sherman Turnpike,
Danbury, Connecticut 06816

FOR BROWN PARTWORKS

Project Editor: Shona Grimbly
Deputy Editor: Rachel Bean
Text Editor: Emily Hill
Designer: Sarah Williams
Picture Research: Veneta Bullen
Maps: Colin Woodman
Design Manager: Lynne Ross
Production: Matt Weyland
Managing Editor: Tim Cooke
Consultant: Stephen A. McKnight
                         University of Florida

Printed and bound in Singapore

ABOUT THIS BOOK

This is one of a set of 10 books that tells the story of the Renaissance—a time of discovery and change in the world. It was during this period—roughly from 1375 to 1575—that adventurous mariners from Europe sailed the vast oceans in tiny ships and found the Americas and new sea routes to the Spice Islands of the East. The influx of gold and silver from the New World and the increase in trade made many merchants and traders in Europe extremely rich. They spent some of their wealth on luxury goods like paintings and gold and silver items for their homes, and this created a new demand for the work of artists of all kinds. Europe experienced a cultural flowering as great artists like Leonardo da Vinci, Michelangelo, and Raphael produced masterpieces that have never been surpassed.

At the same time, scholars were rediscovering the works of the ancient Greek and Roman writers, and this led to a new way of looking at the world based on observation and the importance of the individual. This humanism, together with other new ideas, spread more rapidly than ever before thanks to the development of printing with movable type.

There was upheaval in the church too. Thinkers such as Erasmus and Luther began to question the teachings of the established church, and this eventually led to a breakaway from the Catholic church and the setting up of Protestant churches—an event called the Reformation.

The set focuses on Europe, but it also looks at how societies in other parts of the world such as Africa, China, India, and the Americas were developing, and the ways in which the Islamic and Christian worlds interacted.

The entries in this set are arranged alphabetically and are illustrated with paintings, photographs, drawings, and maps, many from the Renaissance period. Each entry ends with a list of cross-references to other entries in the set, and at the end of each book there is a timeline to help you relate events to one another in time.

There is also a useful "Further Reading" list that includes websites, a glossary of special terms, and an index covering the whole set.

Contents

Volume 10

Technology

During the Middle Ages the technology of the practical and mechanical sciences made slow but significant progress. This continued in Renaissance times, but in a few fields there were epoch-making advances—inventions that made books and knowledge more widely available, revolutionized warfare, and gave Europeans the means to explore, trade with, and eventually dominate distant lands.

Improvements in medieval technology occurred in many areas, ranging from the use of the magnetic compass to the invention of the mechanical clock. In farming, productivity was greatly increased by the introduction of the heavy plow, the horse collar, and the three-year rotation of crops. Spe-

cialized craft tools became more common, along with a range of machines, including lathes, pulleys, mechanical saws, looms, bellows, pumps, and wine presses.

POWER FROM WATER MILLS

Water mills were the main source of mechanical power in the Renaissance period, as they had been in the Middle Ages. A water mill used the power of rushing water to turn a large waterwheel half-submerged in a river or stream. The turning waterwheel was connected by a set of gears to machinery used for various purposes. Water mills often drove millstones to grind grain, bellows for blast furnaces, and forge hammers. They were also used for pressing olives, sawing, and tanning. Windmills were first intro-

Left: An illustration from a 15th-century Dutch manuscript of a water mill. Water mills and windmills (seen in the background) were the main sources of power in Renaissance times. They were used in the countryside for purposes such as grinding grain and pressing olives, and in industry to drive saws, hammers, and bellows for blast furnaces.

Left: A 16th-century painting showing gunpowder being prepared in an armaments factory. The development of gunpowder weapons transformed the nature of warfare.

duced into Europe in the 12th century. They served much the same purposes as water mills and were useful in areas where there was not enough fast flowing water to drive water mills, such as the Netherlands. The Dutch made several improvements to windmills. They invented a hollow postmill in the 15th century that used a two-step gear drive to raise water and built the first wind-driven sawmill in 1592.

THE IMPACT OF GUNPOWDER

In many cases it took a long time for the full effect of technological changes to be felt. Gunpowder, for example, was used in Europe early in the 14th century for firing missiles, but only began to have a major effect in the mid-15th century, when cannon were used in siege warfare. Then, over the course of another 50 years iron replaced stone cannon balls, and the introduction of horse-drawn gun carriages made artillery more mobile. Hand-held guns were first introduced at the beginning of the 15th century, but it was not until the early 16th century that the Spanish produced a much more effective hand-held gun, which was the musket.

The development of artillery had a direct influence on metal technology. The blast furnace began to be more widely used because more iron was needed to make cannon. The blast furnace was a vertical furnace that

TECHNOLOGY IN CHINA

Many of the important technological advances made in Europe during the Renaissance period had been anticipated centuries earlier in China. Paper was widely used there by the fifth century A.D. Printing also began in China, and by the 11th century it was being carried out with movable type. The Chinese invented gunpowder and were using it in warfare by the 11th century; like paper, it was probably copied rather than invented by Europeans. Magnetic compasses were known at an early date, and in the 15th century Chinese vessels—junks—made long voyages all over the Indian Ocean. However, when the Chinese Empire went into decline at the end of the Ming dynasty, Chinese technology stalled at about the same time. In Europe, on the other hand, technological development continued, eventually leading to the Industrial Revolution of the 18th and 19th centuries.

could create the high temperatures needed to produce cast iron by pumping air in under pressure with mechanical bellows. Demand for iron, copper, silver, and coal helped stimulate advances in mining techniques. The German scholar Georg Bauer's manual *De Re Metallica* ("On Metallurgy," 1556) was very influential in spreading ideas and techniques for the mining industry.

During the early Renaissance period there were also technical improvements in industries such as textiles, pottery, and glassmaking. Discoveries were often made by accident or by trial and error rather than by applying scientific principles. Information spread slowly and unevenly, and most industries operated on a small scale.

However, that was to change in the mid-15th century. The introduction of papermaking, and then of printing with movable type, changed the way

---

> ## *Discoveries were often made by accident or by trial and error*

---

that books were made and how they were used. In Europe a papermaking industry started in the 14th century, and it provided the ideal material for a momentous new process—printing. The new printing technology with movable type meant more books were produced much more cheaply, so new ideas could spread rapidly.

TECHNOLOGY AND TRAVEL

Technology had equally dramatic effects on travel and transportation. Canals became more efficient after the

Left: An illustration from a 16th-century German book showing an example of mining technology. The mechanism consists of a series of cogwheels and gears, turned by hand, that operates a scoop to raise material out of the mine.

introduction of locks, and the first coaches appeared in the late 16th century. The biggest change took place on the high seas. Improved sea charts and instruments such as the magnetic compass, astrolabe, and quadrant meant that sailors could navigate better and undertake with confidence much longer voyages than those attempted by medieval mariners.

An important development was the production of oceangoing ships that were suitable for long-distance exploration. In the 15th century the Portuguese created the caravel, a vessel that was sturdy, but also fast and maneuverable thanks to its small size and combination of square and lateen (triangular) sails. These oceangoing vessels enabled Europeans to discover the New World and find sea routes to Asia. Because they were equipped with naval cannon, they also enabled the explorers to dominate the peoples they encountered in those far-flung lands.

SEE ALSO

◆ Arms and Armor
◆ Calendars and Clocks
◆ Fortifications
◆ Glass
◆ Manufacturing
◆ Mining
◆ Navigation
◆ Printing

Textiles

In the Renaissance many different types of textile were made in the countries of western Europe, from woolen and linen fabrics to sumptuous velvets and brocades woven from silk. From the late 14th century the number of people who could afford to buy luxurious clothes and furnishings increased. As towns began to thrive, successful merchants as well as princes and kings wanted expensive textiles to display their wealth and to make their homes more comfortable.

The manufacture of textiles already played a major role in the economies of many countries during the late Middle Ages. England and the Low Countries (present-day Belgium and the Netherlands) in particular grew rich from the production and processing of wool into cloth in the 12th and 13th centuries. The Italian city of Florence also became an important center for finishing and dyeing woolen cloth. Along with Lucca, Genoa, and Venice, Florence also developed into a major center for silk-making. Silk, which is made from the cocoons of the silk moth, was the most precious and sought-after fabric of the time. Until the 14th century Europeans had relied almost completely on trade with China and the Islamic and Byzantine empires for their supply of silk.

Another fabric widely made in the Renaissance was linen, a hard-wearing material suitable for clothing and furnishings. Linen comes from the flax plant, which had been cultivated in western Europe since Roman times. Cotton—which is also made from a plant—was introduced into western Europe in the 14th century, but was not widely available in the Renaissance.

Above: An Italian fresco, or wall painting, showing a fabric shop. It was made in about 1500 to decorate the walls of Issogne Castle in Italy and is from a series of paintings showing daily occupations. On the right of the picture shop assistants are shown measuring out lengths of brightly colored fabric; on the left tailors are cutting out patterns and making clothes.

In the Renaissance several different techniques were used to make textiles, including knitting, felting, and weaving. Knitting was used to make woolen clothes and blankets, as well as fine silk stockings and gloves. Felting, which involves matting and pressing wool fibers together, was especially suitable for warm blankets, rugs, and thick outer cloaks. Weaving was used to create a wide range of different textiles. It was carried out on a large wooden frame called a loom, which had rows of parallel threads, called warps, stretched across it from top to bottom. Threads called wefts were woven in and out of the warps to create pieces of cloth.

Like weaving, textile dyeing was also an important industry in the Middle Ages and Renaissance. The cheapest dyes came from plants that flourished in Europe, such as those belonging to the madder family—from which red dyes were made—and woad, which was used to make blue. However, rarer dyes were very expensive, like the purple made from a shellfish called murex.

WOOL, SILK, AND EMBROIDERIES

Wool was made into a variety of different fabrics, the quality of which depended on how the wool was processed—how it was washed, combed, spun into thread, dyed, woven, and finished. The fabrics ranged from coarse materials used for peasants' clothing to fine, soft materials colored with expensive dyes from which the robes of the wealthy were tailored. Wool was also woven into tapestries, which were luxury textiles with patterns or pictures used for wall hangings and furnishings.

Textiles of all sorts were often decorated with embroidery, a technique in which different stitches and threads are used to sew a pattern

Left: A 15th-century Italian silk textile woven from gold thread with red velvet decoration. The design features a dove, which was the emblem of the powerful Visconti family in Milan for whom the textile was made.

or picture onto a piece of fabric. Embroideries were very popular from the 12th to 14th centuries, before richly patterned silks from Italy became more widely available.

The different types of silk made in Italy and the patterns used to decorate them were influenced by the fabulous examples that were imported from Asia. They included smooth, glossy satins in plain colors and stripes, and damasks—splendid silks with patterns woven into them. Damasks were named after Damascus, the Syrian city where they were first made.

Some of the most sumptuous silk textiles were velvets. They were made by weaving lots of tiny loops of silk into the surface of the cloth. The tops of these loops were then trimmed to leave a soft surface made up of many short threads. Raised patterns were often woven into all types of silk textile using a technique called brocading. Threads made from gold, silver, and brilliantly colored silk were used for the most dazzling brocades and damasks.

SEE ALSO

♦ Antwerp
♦ Bruges
♦ Dress
♦ Guilds
♦ Manufacturing
♦ Tapestry
♦ Trade

Theories of Art and Architecture

In 15th- and 16th-century Italy there was a huge increase in the number of books written about the theory, or ideas, behind art and architecture. They were written by artists who had new aims and values, both for their art and for themselves. The invention of printing meant that their ideas could be transmitted more effectively than ever before, and the theories of artists and architects like Leon Battista Alberti, Andrea Palladio, and Giorgio Vasari soon shaped the way that people throughout Europe created, and thought about, art.

During the Middle Ages almost all art was made for the church. Paintings and sculptures were designed to glorify God and to instruct people in the stories of the Bible. Until the 13th century most artists were members of religious orders and worked in workshops attached to monasteries. They based their art on traditional ways of showing holy figures and Bible stories.

As towns began to flourish in the 13th and 14th centuries, monasteries were no longer the only centers of learning and the arts. Universities were established, and artists set up workshops in towns. Alongside the teachings of the church, scholars began to study the culture of the classical world (ancient Greece and Rome), which placed an increased emphasis on

LEON BATT.ᴬ ALBERTI

human beings and their role in the world. This new way of thinking was known as humanism.

The revival of classical ideas and the growth of humanism influenced the way artists thought about themselves and their work. They became more conscious of how their work related to that of previous artists. Like scholars,

Above: A late 15th-or 16th-century portrait of Leon Battista Alberti, one of the first people to write about Renaissance ideas on art and architecture.

THE COUNCIL OF TRENT AND RELIGIOUS ART

In the 16th century it was not just artists who wrote about theories on painting and sculpture. In response to the rise of Protestantism leaders of the Catholic church began to reform many aspects of Catholicism, including the role of paintings and sculptures in worship. A meeting of church leaders called the Council of Trent (1545–1563) issued guidelines on fitting subjects for religious art and suitable methods of portraying them. They discouraged artists from portraying subjects not described in the Bible and from showing nudes, which they condemned as inappropriate in a church setting.

Italian artists began to study antiquity. They drew and measured the ruins of surviving classical buildings and pieces of sculpture. By the early 15th century artists and architects in Florence started to base their work on classical examples. They admired the order and grandeur of classical buildings as well as the naturalism (lifelike appearance) and portrayal of the unclothed human form that were important features of classical sculpture.

The first person to promote these values in art was Leon Battista Alberti (1404–1472), a wealthy churchman, writer, and architect. In 1436 he wrote *Della Pittura* ("On Painting"), in which he urged painters to study classical art and to base their work on a careful observation of nature. He wrote that they should aim to re-create the appearance of the world in their paintings. The study of nature— particularly the human form—became a fundamental part of Renaissance artistic practice.

Both Alberti and Leonardo da Vinci (1452–1518) stressed that artists

Left: **Apelles and the Cobbler** *by Giorgio Vasari. The painting illustrates a story about the ancient Greek painter Apelles that stresses the importance of creating lifelike art. A cobbler points out to Apelles that he has incorrectly painted a sandal; on being told of his mistake, Apelles repaints the sandal right away. The story influenced Renaissance artists.*

needed to understand the underlying structure of objects, and not just the surface appearances. Leonardo carried out exhaustive researches into the natural world, including dissections to understand better how bodies worked. Alberti laid down the rules for linear perspective, a mathematical system that enabled painters to create an accurate impression of three-dimensional space in their pictures.

CREATING BEAUTY

The goal of Renaissance artists was to achieve beauty, and like classical artists they aimed to show it through their portrayal of the human form. They recognized that the beauty they so admired in classical sculptures did not come from directly copying nature. Alberti recommended that artists should select only the most beautiful things they saw. He and many later artists also suggested systems of ideal proportions—mathematical formulas to help artists show the human body with pleasing proportions.

By the 16th century artists and theorists placed more emphasis on the role of the artist's imagination in creating beauty. Michelangelo saw the artist's creativity as the source of beauty. The painter and art historian Giorgio Vasari shared this view. His book *Lives of the Artists* (1550) was the first history of 15th- and 16th-century Italian art and remains a key source of information on Renaissance ideas.

THE STATUS OF ARTISTS

As artists reassessed their aims in art, they also reassessed their social status. They wanted to be regarded as intellectuals, not craftsmen. In their writings Alberti, Leonardo, Vasari, and the sculptors Lorenzo Ghiberti and Benvenuto Cellini all emphasized the

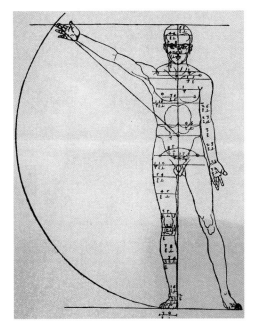

Left: A diagram by the German artist Albrecht Dürer (1471–1528) showing the ideal proportions, or measurements, he devised for showing the human body. Dürer visited Italy on many occasions and was much influenced by the latest ideas of Italian artists like Leonardo da Vinci.

intellectual aspect of artistic practice, stressing that their art was founded on their knowledge of antiquity, science, and mathematics.

Alberti was the first person to write about Renaissance ideas on architecture. From the 1440s he compiled *De re aedificatoria* ("On Architecture"), a comprehensive book describing how architects could adapt the rules of classical architecture to the needs of the present day. It was based on his study of classical ruins and a book written by the Roman architect Vitruvius, the only complete work on classical architecture to survive into the Renaissance.

Other architects soon followed Alberti's example. From 1537 to 1551 Sebastiano Serlio wrote *L'Architettura* ("Architecture"), which provided practical information for designing in the classical style. In 1570 Andrea Palladio published *Quattro libri dell'architettura* ("Four Books on Architecture"). These books were soon translated into other languages, enabling architects in countries far away from Italy to design buildings in the Italian Renaissance style.

SEE ALSO

♦ Alberti
♦ Antiquities
♦ Architecture
♦ Classicism
♦ Drawing
♦ Ghiberti
♦ Human Form
   in Art
♦ Leonardo da
   Vinci
♦ Michelangelo
♦ Naturalism
♦ Painting
♦ Palladio
♦ Perspective
♦ Religious
   Themes in Art
♦ Renaissance,
   Idea of
♦ Sculpture
♦ Vasari

Tintoretto

The Venetian painter Tintoretto (1518–1594) worked in a highly individual and dramatic style, and his pictures are full of religious intensity. He painted quickly and developed a loose, sketchy technique based on strong contrasts of light and shadow. His paintings also appear to be full of movement, with the figures shown in exaggerated poses, often from dramatic angles.

Tintoretto's real name was Jacopo Robusti, but he was given the nickname "Tintoretto" (Italian for "little dyer") because his father worked as a cloth dyer (*tintore*). Tintoretto was largely self-taught as a painter, though scholars think that he probably studied briefly under the greatest Venetian artist of the time, Titian.

EARLY INFLUENCES

Tintoretto is said to have written his formula for artistic success on the wall of his studio: "The drawing of Michelangelo and the coloring of Titian." Michelangelo's powerful, dynamic style was based on his talent as a draftsman, while Titian's rich, glowing paintings were based on his use of color and loose brushwork. Tintoretto's work combined the approaches of both these artists.

By 1539 Tintoretto had opened his own workshop in Venice. Ten years later he established his reputation as the most exciting young artist of the day with the large oil painting *Saint Mark Rescuing the Slave* (1548). It was painted for the Scuola di San Marco,

one of a number of charitable organizations called *scuole*, which were devoted to good works. The painting shows Saint Mark coming down from heaven to rescue a slave who has been condemned to death for his Christian beliefs. Tintoretto painted the subject in a startlingly original way. He used strong light and shade to add drama to the scene, and showed Saint Mark hurtling downward while the onlookers draw back in astonishment.

CONTROVERSY AND FAME

Initially the *scuola* rejected Tintoretto's painting—they later accepted it when Tintoretto had established his reputation—but the incident generated so much publicity that many powerful people and organizations soon wanted him to paint for them. Unlike Titian, who traveled widely, Tintoretto spent his working life in Venice. His vivid style was well suited to portraying miraculous stories from the Bible, and

Below: **Saint Mark Rescuing the Slave** *(1548), the painting that established Tintoretto's reputation. It shows a story from the legend of Saint Mark in which he rescues a Christian slave condemned to death. As Saint Mark soars down from heaven, his miraculous powers cause the ropes binding the slave to come undone and the instruments used to torture him to shatter.*

Left: **The Last Supper (1592–1594) was one of the last paintings Tintoretto made. It sums up his intensely spiritual style with its dynamic diagonal arrangement, dramatic lighting, and use of unearthly colors.**

they became his main theme. He also painted portraits and scenes from classical mythology.

Tintoretto was very ambitious and often ruthless in getting work. In 1564 a competition was held to find an artist to decorate the Scuola San Rocco. Invited artists were asked to bring a sketch for a painting of Saint Roch (San Rocco in Italian) to go on the ceiling of the *scuola*. On the day of the competition Tintoretto arrived empty-handed. He pointed up to the ceiling, where he had somehow managed to have his finished painting installed. His tactics generated much bad feeling, but he won the competition, and over the next 20 years painted some of his greatest works for the *scuola*.

Following Titian's death in 1574, Tintoretto became the most acclaimed artist in Venice. During the last years of his life Tintoretto's style became even more individual, as can be seen in the intense and powerful *The Last Supper* (1592–1594), completed in the year of his death. Tintoretto's work influenced many later artists, especially El Greco, a Greek painter who spent most of his working life in Spain.

NOVEL TECHNIQUE

Tintoretto used an unusual method in order to help him work out ideas for his huge paintings. He made small wax and clay models of the figures he wanted to paint and arranged them on a miniature stage. Sometimes he suspended them by strings or wires—that is probably how he figured out how to paint the figure of Saint Mark in *Saint Mark Rescuing the Slave*. He also experimented with lighting the models from different directions, a practice that influenced the strong light and shade in his paintings. Most artists worked out their ideas in drawings and painted studies, but only a few such studies by Tintoretto survive.

SEE ALSO

♦ Michelangelo
♦ Religious Themes in Art
♦ Titian
♦ Venice

Titian

Tiziano Vecellio (about 1487–1576), known as Titian, was the greatest 16th-century painter in Venice. Influenced by the Venetian painters Giovanni Bellini and Giorgione, he explored fresh ways of portraying subjects and also of using oil paint, at first exploiting its brilliant colors and later developing an increasingly free technique. Titian's inventive and magnificent handling of religious subjects, scenes from classical (ancient Greek and Roman) myths, and portraits made him one of the most sought-after painters in Europe.

Titian was born in the town of Pieve di Cadore, north of Venice. In later life he claimed that he was born in 1477—which would have made him 99 years old when he died—but most scholars think Titian exaggerated his age and that he was probably born around 1487. As a young man, Titian went to Venice, where he trained in the workshop of Giovanni Bellini. He later worked with another gifted young artist, Giorgione.

Titian was strongly influenced by Giorgione's style, especially the dreamlike mood of his paintings and the way he showed subjects from classical

Left: Titian's Bacchus and Ariadne (1520–1523), one of a series of paintings made to decorate a room in Duke Alfonso d'Este's castle in Ferrara, Italy. It shows Bacchus leaping from his chariot to greet Ariadne. The cheetahs drawing the chariot are based on animals in Alfonso's private zoo, while the male figure entwined with snakes is based on the Laocoön, a classical sculpture.

myths. Because the two artists worked in such similar styles, scholars have found it difficult to decide which of them painted a number of unsigned pictures. The two artists were working together when Giorgione died in 1510. Titian then began to make his name as an independent artist with paintings like his three frescoes (paintings made on wet, or "fresh," plaster) *The Miracles of Saint Anthony* in Padua. He enjoyed increasing success, and when Giovanni Bellini died in 1516, Titian became the leading artist in Venice.

DRAMATIC NEW WORKS

From 1516 to 1518 Titian painted *The Assumption of the Virgin* (see page 43) for the church of Santa Maria Gloriosa dei Frari in Venice. It is a huge painting, with a powerful composition (arrangement) inspired by the painter Raphael and made even more dramatic by Titian's use of color. Titian painted bright golden light streaming down from the heavens and gave the most important figures brilliant red robes to make them stand out.

Titian used a similarly inventive approach in another religious painting, *The Pesaro Madonna* (1519–1526), which shows Mary and the baby Jesus with saints and the Pesaro family, who paid for the painting. Unlike most works of this kind, which showed Mary seated on a throne in the center of the picture, Titian placed her to one side of the painting amid a setting of steps and huge columns outside a church.

PAINTING CLASSICAL MYTHS

Between 1518 and 1523 Titian painted a series of pictures with mythological subjects for Alfonso d'Este, duke of Ferrara. Many art historians consider one of these paintings, *Bacchus and Ariadne* (1520–1523), to be his greatest

PORTRAIT PAINTER

Titian's skill as a portrait painter was one of the reasons that his services were in such demand. He painted Europe's great princes and churchmen as they wanted to be seen, as wealthy and powerful men. With his eye for rich color and the freedom and flourish of his style, he painted his subjects in shining suits of armor and sumptuous clothing. At the same time, he sensitively captured the features of their faces. He also flattered his sitters—when he painted the Holy Roman emperor Charles V he played down the emperor's large jaw. Charles was so impressed with Titian's portraits that he knighted him.

Above: Titian's portrait of the writer Pietro Aretino (1545). By devoting a large part of the portrait to Aretino's lavish velvet robes, Titian adds to the magnificence of the image.

work. It shows Bacchus, god of wine, leaping from a chariot to greet Ariadne, daughter of the king of Crete, whom he later married. The lively portrayal of Bacchus's reveling followers, the glowing landscape, and the brilliant colors all appealed to the Renaissance idea of what the classical world had been like.

In the 1530s Titian painted another very influential painting that took its subject from classical myth: the *Venus of Urbino* (about 1538). It shows Venus, goddess of love, as a nude (unclothed) woman lying on a bed looking alluringly out of the picture. Titian painted many more pictures like the *Venus of Urbino* to hang in the private rooms of male patrons. His later paintings of classical subjects were increasingly sensual portrayals of nude figures, especially the mythological paintings he made for King Philip II of Spain in the 1550s and 1560s.

CHANGING STYLE

Titian enjoyed outstanding success in the 1530s. He was courted by Europe's most powerful rulers, including the Holy Roman emperor Charles V—and later his son King Philip II of Spain—as well as popes and Italian princes. However, his life was also touched by great sadness when his wife Cecilia died in 1530. At this time, Titian's style changed. Instead of bright, contrasting colors, he started to work in a more tonal way, basing his style on light and shade. At the same, time his brush-marks and the way he applied oil paint grew freer and more expressive. Although traditionally artists applied oil paint in many thin layers, Titian often applied oil paint very thickly, a technique called "impasto."

LATE WORKS

Titian's style continued to develop after 1550. In his later years the figures in his pictures became less solid. His works were filled with hazy, golden light and painted with even freer brushstrokes.

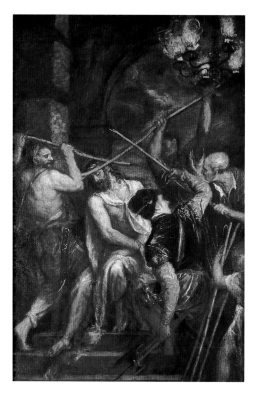

Left: **Crowning with Thorns (1570–1576), one of Titian's last paintings. It shows Christ being beaten by soldiers, who have placed a crown of thorns on his head. The painting is typical of Titian's late style, with its freely applied paint and use of light and dark shades rather than bright colors.**

The Italian artist and writer Giorgio Vasari commented that Titian's new works were "executed with bold, sweeping strokes and in patches of color, with the result that they cannot be viewed from near by, but appear perfect at a distance." Titian's late style can be seen in the mythological paintings he made for Philip II, which Titian himself described as *poesie*, or poems in paint.

In the last years of his life Titian continued to paint great works, including *The Annunciation* (1560–1565) and *Crowning with Thorns* (1570–1576). He was working on a pietà (a painting showing Mary with the dead Christ) in 1576, when he died on August 27. Along with Leonardo da Vinci, Raphael, and Michelangelo, Titian was one of the greatest artists of the Renaissance. His new approach to religious and mythological paintings, his powerful portraits, and his use of oil paint shaped the work of generations of later artists.

SEE ALSO

♦ Bellini, Giovanni
♦ Giorgione
♦ Mythological Art
♦ Painting
♦ Painting Techniques and Materials
♦ Philip II
♦ Portraiture
♦ Tintoretto
♦ Venice
♦ Veronese

Towns

In the Middle Ages most towns were little more than overgrown villages, often clustering around the walls of a castle. They might have fewer than 2,000 inhabitants, who were dependent on the produce of the local countryside. Some of these towns would have markets for farmers. Toward the end of the medieval period some towns started to grow in size as there was an increase in trade and prosperity. Populations grew with an influx of craftsmen, artisans, merchants, and tradespeople. Some small market towns, such as Norwich in eastern England, grew rapidly to become major regional centers.

As towns became centers of manufacturing and long-distance trade, people from the countryside flocked to them in the hope of finding work. By the early 16th century the size of populations living in towns had increased dramatically. The very largest towns—Naples and Paris—had more than 200,000 citizens, while Venice, Milan, Genoa, and Florence had 100,000 each. Smaller towns had between 10,000 and 40,000 citizens.

Many of the large urban centers sought to free themselves from their overlords and became self-governing. The merchants and tradesmen who made up a large section of the citizens elected their own town government from among their number—in Italy this type of town government was called a commune, while in England it was called a corporation. These

independent towns became very wealthy, which attracted yet more citizens to them.

Many towns had been built on existing Roman foundations, but they frequently diverged from their original, regular Roman grid pattern. Other towns had grown organically from villages and had curving streets, narrow alleys, and cramped courtyards. Renaissance towns dating from the Middle Ages were usually surrounded by fortified walls. By the 16th century these walls were no defense against heavy artillery, and they gradually fell into disrepair.

Some towns grew up around a focal point, such as a castle or monastery, and originally developed to service

Above: The town hall and public square in Cortona, Italy. In the 15th and 16th centuries the town hall was the seat of the town government. Once a week local farmers, traders, craftsmen, and townspeople would flock to the market that was held in the square in front of the town hall.

TOWN GOVERNMENT

As towns became more prosperous, their citizens fought to establish their independence from an often remote overlord. In Italy town communes were formed, while in England the goal was to become a municipal corporation, established by royal charter. Many communes and corporations were based on medieval guilds, which often became rich and powerful, and endowed the town with land and charitable institutions, such as hospitals and alms-houses. The privileges of belonging to the commune or corporation only extended to the "freemen" of the town. Freemen were originally tradespeople—merchants, artisans, stallholders, and innkeepers. Membership in this select group was strictly controlled. Although all freemen were technically members of the governing body, in reality towns were governed by an inner group. In England it consisted of a mayor, a body of aldermen and councillors, and a town clerk, who was responsible for keeping records. The corporation maintained law and order within the town with the help of a sheriff, beadles, and marshals. Towns were governed with elaborate ceremony. Each town official had imposing robes, and the mayor carried a sword and mace as symbols of office. On Sundays civic dignitaries paraded to church in full regalia. The town corporation would often put on lavish entertainments and banquets as a way of celebrating the town's wealth and status.

them. The walls of castle towns frequently linked up with the castle itself, creating an impregnable fortress. Alternatively, a town might have been laid out on a new site, with straight, parallel streets and regularly de-marcated plots, all measured and mapped by surveyors. Some towns, such as Krakow in Poland, combined various forms. The center of Krakow was the castle, set high on a crag above the Vistula River. An organic medieval settlement grew beneath the castle, a rabbit warren of narrow, winding streets. By the 14th century a planned town had been added, which was laid out on a grid pattern, with broad parallel streets and open squares.

Left: A view of Paris, the capital of France, as it was in the early 16th century. The city was surrounded by a fortified wall and a moat, and the streets were laid out in a fairly regular pattern. The center of the city was an island on the Seine River, connected to the mainland by four bridges.

There was at least one marketplace in most Renaissance towns, which was the focus of the town's commercial life. Once a week the market was alive with farmers, traders, craftsmen, townspeople, and probably pickpockets, and the inns and taverns that lined the market square did a roaring business. Frequently the town hall, seat of the town's government, and guildhall (which was the administrative center for the merchant and craft guilds) fronted the market square. Churches also provided a communal focus for the townspeople.

LIVING CLOSE TOGETHER

Separate streets or quarters were devoted to a particular trade, and industrial quarters were placed together, away from the town center. Housing in most Renaissance towns was tightly packed. Narrow-fronted, gabled houses jostled together for space and light in narrow streets. The houses, usually three or four stories high, often jutted out over the street. Drainage from the houses led to cesspools (for collecting sewage) and leaching fields. Nightsoil men had the task of cleaning the cesspools. Even so, waste seeped into the ground and back into the water supply, which was often contaminated—in many towns water was drawn directly from badly polluted rivers. Refuse was frequently dumped directly into the streets. Streets were unlighted and dangerous after dark. Town authorities often imposed a night curfew; and although night watchmen patrolled the streets, crime inevitably increased under cover of darkness.

Fire was a constant danger. Houses were often built of wood, and people cooked over open hearths. Once a fire started, it could rage uncontrollably for days. The only way to halt its progress was to create firebreaks by demolishing buildings that lay in its path. Sometimes whole towns were obliterated; in 1518 the French town of Armentières suffered a terrible fire—out of a total of 1,300 houses only three of them survived

The cramped and unsanitary (dirty) conditions in which most townspeople lived encouraged the spread of infectious diseases, such as plague and typhoid. People living in towns in the 16th century could expect, on average, to live no longer than 25 to 30 years. In fact, the populations of most towns would have been continually declining if it had not been for the steady flow of people from the countryside who moved to the towns in search of a more prosperous life.

Left: A narrow street in Bevagna, Italy. Because space in Renaissance towns was limited, houses were built three or four stories high and very close together, making the streets dark and narrow.

Trade

Most people lived and worked on the land in the Renaissance period and rarely went farther than their local market. All the same, long-distance trade became increasingly important. Markets, fairs, and towns flourished, and money was used more widely. Transportation both by sea and on land continued to be slow and dangerous, so trade was risky; but new banking arrangements made business between merchants in different countries simpler. The great voyages of discovery led to an expansion of trade across the world.

International trade became well established in Europe between 1000 and 1350 A.D. Cities in Flanders (present-day Belgium and parts of France and the Netherlands) and northern Italy became great manufacturing centers, and towns across Europe grew in size and importance. Trade with Asia also flourished as networks of merchants transported and exchanged goods along ancient trade routes.

Italy became the leading commercial nation, and great Italian banking houses such as those of the Bardi and the Peruzzi were established. The Italian cities of Florence and Venice minted the first gold coins since the time of the Roman Empire, and merchants and bankers began to devise credit arrangements that made it possible to do business without carrying large amounts of money over long distances. Merchants sent trusted agents to live abroad to carry out their business for them.

There was an economic crisis in the 14th century partly brought about by the collapse of the Italian banks and growing insecurity on the trade routes across Asia. From 1347 a plague, the Black Death, swept across Europe, killing up to a third of the population. The economic consequences were severe, but trading patterns changed very little. In fact, the trading empire of Venice became even more successful, and new international banks emerged, such as the Medici bank in Florence.

The driving force behind trade was the demand for goods that were either not produced locally or were not available in sufficient quantities. Although spices from Asia were more glamorous, grain was the most vital of commodities traded in Renaissance Europe. It was widely grown but was often in short supply either because of bad local harvests, or because it was needed to feed the populations of large cities. Getting more grain by trade was slow; it took up to a year to transport grain from eastern to western Europe.

THE BALTIC

Grain was one reason why the Baltic was a major trading region. From the late 13th century trade in the Baltic was largely controlled by the Hanseatic League (the Hansa), an organization of trading cities in northern Europe. The Hansa merchants had access to the vast grain-growing lands of Poland and Germany, which could supply grain when harvests in other areas failed. Other goods, from herring, timber, and iron to furs, amber, and honey, were traded via the Baltic with the rest of Europe. Merchants aimed to monopolize (have exclusive rights to) trade where possible, and the Hansa towns were even prepared to go to war to defend their privileges if necessary.

The Baltic region imported manufactured goods in return for foodstuffs and raw materials. The most

important of these were textiles. Flanders and northern Italy were the great manufacturing centers of the Renaissance; the raw materials were supplied by England, Ireland, and Spain. North–south trade routes brought prosperity to other parts of Europe, including southern Germany, where armor from Augsburg and Nuremberg was in great demand.

The Mediterranean was a center of intensive trading activity, dominated

Above: A 16th-century painting of a cloth fair in the Netherlands, which was a major region for textile manufacturing in the Renaissance. Manufactured goods were sold or exchanged at markets and fairs.

by the economic power of northern Italy. The Italians had few natural resources, but they excelled as textile manufacturers and international bankers. Merchants from Genoa and Venice controlled much of the trade in the region. Trade with Asia was another source of great riches for the Italians. From the 14th century routes across Asia were closed to Europeans due to the unstable policial situation, but the Venetians established trading posts at the eastern Mediterranean end of the transcontinental routes. The goods brought to Europe by Italian merchants included spices, silks, and many other luxurious items.

THE FLANDERS FLEET

For northern merchants one of the great events of the year was the arrival of a fleet of galleys from Venice. They first came in 1317 after a quarrel with France closed the overland routes to Venetian goods. Normally galleys operated in the relatively quiet waters of the Mediterranean, but on this occasion the Venetian fleet sailed through the Mediterranean, the Strait of Gibraltar, and the Atlantic, and on to England and the Netherlands; it was probably the longest trading voyage undertaken by Europeans since Roman times. The Venetians brought cargoes of spices, sugar, cotton, silk, and other luxury goods, returning with commodities such as English wool and metal and Flemish textiles. The Flanders Fleet sailed for the next two hundred years.

SEA ROUTE TO INDIA

Bringing goods overland from Asia was very expensive. Transportation costs were high, and heavy taxes had to be paid for transporting merchandise through Ottoman-controlled territory. From the 1420s the Portuguese began to explore down the coast of Africa hoping to find a sea route to Asia. They also wanted to trade directly in sub-Saharan Africa, rather than dealing with the Arab middlemen in north Africa. They established a series of fortified trading posts along the African coast, from which they traded leather, textiles, weapons, and wine in exchange for gold, ivory, and slaves. In 1498 Vasco da Gama reached India by

Left: A 19th-century woodcut showing the Portuguese explorer Vasco da Gama handing the ruler of Calicut in India a letter from the king of Portugal in 1498. Da Gama's discovery of a sea route to India meant that the Portuguese could trade directly with Asia, bypassing the expensive land route controlled by the Ottomans.

sea and established the lucrative Portuguese seaborne spice trade.

These voyages of discovery and Columbus's discovery of the Americas in 1492 allowed Europeans to trade over much of the world. Products from Asia became cheaper and more easily available. The Americas supplied a range of new commodities (potatoes, tomatoes, corn, tobacco, chocolate) and the promise of huge quantities of silver, gold, and sugar. The trade in African slaves was at first undertaken to supply Portugal's labor shortage, but was soon expanded to provide a mass labor force in the New World.

STIFLING CONTROL

The discoveries would have had more impact if the Portuguese and Spanish crowns had not exercised a stifling control over colonial trade. Neither took advantage of their economic opportunities. From the 1540s huge amounts of silver flowed into Spain, only to be squandered on wars. The result was to pump silver bullion into the European economy, but in such large quantities that it helped fuel a steep rise in prices.

For most of the 16th century trade expanded rapidly. German bankers replaced Italians in importance, but northern Italy remained a major economic and financial center. Despite the new seaborne trade with Asia, Venice remained prosperous, and Mediterranean trade flourished. The Low Countries (present-day Belgium and the Netherlands) grew in prosperity. Later in the 16th century the newly independent Dutch emerged as a commercial and seafaring nation. England too began to develop into a strong seafaring power. By the 17th century a process had begun that would shift economic power away from the Mediterranean and other traditional centers to the western European nations that were now starting to occupy the center of an almost world-wide network of trade.

Above: A painting of Antwerp's harbor and fish market as it was in about 1600. Antwerp was the largest and wealthiest city in northern Europe during the 16th century because of its importance as a center of trade.

SEE ALSO

♦ Antwerp
♦ Banking
♦ Bruges
♦ Capitalism
♦ Exploration
♦ Free Cities
♦ Manufacturing
♦ Merchants
♦ Portugal
♦ Venice
♦ Wealth

Transportation

The transportation systems of the Renaissance were little better than those of the Middle Ages. For most people travel was a slow and laborious process along badly maintained and bumpy roads. Horses or horse-drawn wagons were the normal means of travel, though some bulky goods traveled along rivers in boats and barges. Despite the inefficiency of road travel, diplomatic news traveled fast, and many people, such as monarchs, merchants, priests, and soldiers, managed to travel vast distances across Europe and Asia.

The main passenger vehicle was the four-wheeled horse-drawn wagon, an adaptation of the peasant cart. Various improvements were introduced: wagons were covered, seats were bolted in, and in some cases straps were used to suspend the passenger compartment. This innovation eased the bone-rattling jolts, but produced a swaying motion that could cause travel sickness. Progress was slow; a wagon traveled no more than 20 miles (32km) a day. In 1518 the humanist scholar Erasmus traveled from Cologne to Aachen and complained, "I arrived exhausted from the shaking of the carriage, which was so trying to me . . . that I should have preferred sitting on my horse."

ON HORSEBACK

Renaissance travelers who could afford it traveled on horseback. A rider could cover up to 50 miles (80km) a day along a reasonably good road. Nevertheless, long days of horseback riding were exhausting and uncomfortable. A 16th-century German merchant complained, "I have had so

Left: A four-wheeled horse-drawn wagon full of passengers, shown in a 16th-century painting. A journey by road was slow and uncomfortable—the wagon swayed from side to side and jolted over potholes, leaving the passengers exhausted at the end of the day.

little respite that my bottom has been constantly a-fire from the saddle." Improvements appeared gradually. Inns, posting stations, and horse relay stations along the way made travel faster and more comfortable. With frequent changes of horse a messenger could cover long distances at a fast gallop. International and diplomatic news traveled relatively quickly across the continent; for example, on November 15, 1565, Spanish soldiers pillaged and burned the town of Antwerp. Just three weeks later, on December 4, news of this event was recorded in the diary of a local squire in a remote corner of Cornwall in southwest England. News could travel

---

Diplomatic news traveled relatively quickly

---

between Rome and the cities of Florence and Naples in just three days, while it took 26 days for news to be carried between Rome and Madrid.

Roads were created haphazardly. They were built, maintained, and paid for by local taxes, and their state of repair varied considerably. In some regions local conditions made the problem worse; in marshy lowland areas roads were rutted, bumpy, and waterlogged for several months a year. Even well-maintained roads were rough and potholed.

TRANSPORTATION BY WATER

By 1500 fully rigged ships, with three masts and as many as eight sails, were plying the world's oceans, transporting commodities such as Asian spices and South American gold to Europe. However, within the continent of Europe

water transportation was much less advanced. Some rivers were used for the bulk transportation of goods such as building stone, timber, and grain. In some cases barges and oared boats just traveled downriver and were broken up for timber when they reached their destination. But on large rivers, like the Rhine, Elbe, and lower Seine, a considerable amount of long-distance river traffic passed back and forth. On some rivers, like the Rhine, ships were even able to travel under sail (and therefore much more quickly), since the rivers were wide enough to allow them to tack back and forth.

Rivers were also used for local transportation; for example, some peasants took their farm produce to market in small boats. River transportation was restricted by natural and artificial obstacles, such as shallows, floods, unpredictable currents, mills, and weirs. But even though boats had to pay local tolls to use waterways, it was cheaper to transport goods by water than by land. Canals were only used in the lowlands of Holland and did not appear elsewhere in Europe until the 17th century.

Above: Boats taking on passengers, shown in **The Landing Place,** *a painting by Jan Bruegel the Elder (1568–1625). River travel was cheaper and much more comfortable than traveling by road.*

SEE ALSO

♦ Communications
♦ Merchants
♦ Ships
♦ Trade

Uccello

Paolo Uccello (about 1396–1475) created some of the most distinctive paintings of the 15th century. In them he combined a feeling for pattern and bright color inspired by the International Gothic—a highly decorative style that was popular when he was a young man—and an interest in perspective, a newly discovered mathematical system that helped artists show the three-dimensional world on the flat surface of a picture. It is for his daring experiments with perspective that Uccello is best remembered.

Uccello was born in Florence in about 1396, the son of a barber. At the age of about 10 he was employed in the workshop of the great Florentine sculptor Ghiberti, where he helped on the bronze doors Ghiberti was making for the baptistery of Florence Cathedral. In 1415 he became a member of the painters' guild—an organization that regulated painters' work and training—and 10 years later he went to Venice, where he worked on mosaics in the church of Saint Mark's.

Returning to Florence in about 1430, Uccello found that the latest fashion among artists involved attempting to create a new naturalistic, or lifelike, style. One of the devices artists used to help them achieve this aim was linear perspective, a technique that involves creating a sense of depth in a picture. Before the Renaissance artists had been aware that trees in the distance should be shown smaller than

Left: Uccello's painting Saint George and the Dragon *(about 1460). It shows how Uccello combined the Gothic style—seen in the flat way he painted the maiden and the fanciful cave mouth—with perspective. He used this mathematical system to make the horse appear solid and to create a sense of space by arranging the plants on a grid.*

THE BATTLE OF SAN ROMANO

Uccello painted three large paintings of the battle of San Romano, which had taken place on June 1, 1432, when the Florentine army defeated its Sienese enemies. The paintings emphasize the splendor of the soldiers—their horses and armor, crested helmets, and bristling lances—rather than the goriness of warfare. In the central panel shown here, Uccello portrays the decisive moment in the battle when the Sienese commander, Bernardino della Carda, is lanced by a Florentine soldier. Uccello's concern for pattern and shape can be seen in the straight lines of the lances and in details such as the dog and hares running through the fields. His interest in perspective and foreshortening are evident in the way the horses are shown, particularly the rearing white horse at left and the bucking brown horse at right.

Left: **The Battle of San Romano** (1456–1460), *one of a set of three paintings made by Uccello commemorating the Florentine victory over Sienese troops in 1432.*

those nearby. However, they had not devised a system to work out the different sizes. The artist Filippo Brunelleschi is credited with figuring out the rules early in the 15th century.

Perspective fascinated Uccello, and he began to explore foreshortening—a way of showing objects as they appear from a particular angle. For example, if an artist was painting a man who had his arm outstretched toward him, he would emphasize the size and position of the hand, which would appear large and block out most of the arm behind.

Uccello was soon given a chance to try out the new techniques when he was asked to paint a fresco com-memorating Sir John Hawkwood, an English soldier who had fought in Italy as a mercenary. Uccello showed Hawk-wood sitting on a horse and painted him to appear like a three-dimensional carved statue.

In about 1445 Uccello left Florence for Padua, although two years later he was back working on frescoes showing scenes from the Old Testament story of Noah and the flood. In the following years he painted *Saint George and the Dragon* (about 1460) and *The Battle of San Romano* (1456–1460), his last great works. The remaining years of Uccello's life were marked by ill health and money problems, and he died in 1475.

SEE ALSO

- Arms and Armor
- Brunelleschi
- Condottieri
- Ghiberti
- Gothic Art
- Masaccio
- Naturalism
- Perspective

Universities

The first universities were founded in the Middle Ages and developed from the cathedral schools of the Catholic church. They spread rapidly through Italy, France, England, and Spain. Their numbers increased dramatically in the 14th century, and the traditional medieval courses of study were gradually replaced by the new humanist learning of the Renaissance.

Bologna in Italy was the first university, founded in the 11th century. It was followed in the late 12th century by universities in Paris, France, Oxford and Cambridge in England, and others in Spain, France, Italy, and Portugal. The universities originally took mainly churchmen as students and taught subjects at a more advanced level than church and monastic schools. They were licensed by popes or monarchs, who authorized the masters to examine students and award them degrees. Universities were self-governing and also self-financing. Students paid fees; and if they were dissatisfied, they could go elsewhere. Oxford University was founded after a student walkout from the University of Paris; Cambridge University in turn originated with disgruntled Oxford students.

Teaching and books were in Latin, which was the international language of scholarship and religion. The

Below: A view of All Soul's College, part of Oxford University in England. Oxford was one of the earliest universities and dates from the late 12th century.

students of a university often came from many countries. There was a great age of expansion in the late 15th century, when 50 new universities were founded all across Europe.

Most universities had a number of separate faculties or departments devoted to different subjects. Students usually began with an arts degree. The first stage, known as the *trivium*, consisted of grammar, rhetoric, and logic—the arts of language and argument. It was followed by the *quadrivium*, which comprised astronomy, arithmetic, geometry, and music. The student then went on to more advanced courses in medicine, law, or theology (the study of religion).

RENAISSANCE SCHOLARSHIP

From the 15th century the humanist new learning of the Renaissance began to influence universities. Its followers were generally critical of the approach of the old university tradition and wanted to study important texts for themselves. In particular, the study of Greek gained a new importance through the discovery of ancient texts. This resulted in new insights into the New Testament, which, though it was originally written in Greek, had for centuries been known in the West only in Latin translation.

During the early Renaissance period many universities remained conservative in outlook, and in Italy humanist ideas mainly advanced through academies (associations of scholars) and courts. But as early as 1395 Florence University acquired a professor of Greek, and the foundation of Ferrara University in 1447 was primarily the work of a famous humanist educator, Guarino da Verona. By the 16th century the new learning was making its mark even in England,

where from 1511 to 1514 the great Dutch humanist Desiderius Erasmus was professor of Greek at the University of Cambridge.

INFLUENCE OF PROTESTANTISM

The Protestant Reformation of the 16th century strengthened the conservative forces in many existing Catholic universities, which suspected humanist studies of encouraging heresy (ideas contrary to the teachings of the church). However, some universities favored Protestantism. The intellectual center of Lutheranism was Wittenberg University, which was founded in 1502. The university of Marburg, founded in 1527, was the first of a number of new specifically Protestant foundations. Later, other universities were also established as part of the Catholic Counter Reformation, notably by the Jesuits. These universities produced the churchmen, statesmen, officials, and thinkers of a Europe deeply divided along religious lines.

Above: A map showing the main universities in Europe at the beginning of the 15th century.

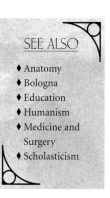

SEE ALSO

♦ Anatomy
♦ Bologna
♦ Education
♦ Humanism
♦ Medicine and Surgery
♦ Scholasticism

Urbino

The city of Urbino lies in a region of central Italy called the Marches. During the 15th century the city became one of the most important centers of Renaissance culture, famous for the artists and scholars who worked there as well as for its most brilliant ruler, Duke Federigo da Montefeltro (1420–1482).

The Montefeltro family first ruled Urbino in the early 13th century. Before that time the city was part of the Papal States, the territories in central Italy ruled by the pope. The Montefeltro counts were often great soldiers. They used their military skills to support the cause of the Holy Roman Empire, which was then fighting the papacy for control of Italy. The poet Dante Alighieri mentions Guido da Montefeltro (1255–1298) in his book *The Divine Comedy*, which describes

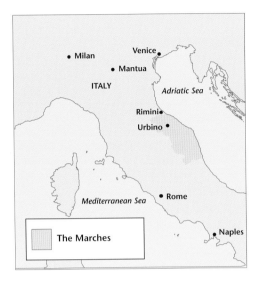

Left: A map showing Urbino and the area of the Marches in Italy. The Montefeltro dukes ruled most of the Marches region.

the count burning in hell as a punishment for his crafty ways.

At the end of the 14th century Antonio da Montefeltro (died 1404) finally made peace with the pope and was able to extend his lands far into the Marches. As allies of the papacy, the Montefeltro counts fought the

Below: A view of Urbino. Federigo da Montefeltro's great Renaissance palace can be identified by its twin towers and three balconies, one on top of the other.

AN IDEAL PRINCE

Many of Federigo da Montefeltro's contemporaries saw him as the ideal Renaissance prince. He was not only a brave soldier but also a highly cultured patron who invited scholars and artists to work at his court. He was a friend of one of the leading thinkers and writers about art and architecture, Leon Battista Alberti, whose ideas influenced the new buildings Federigo commissioned in Urbino. As a young boy, he spent two years as a hostage at the court of the marquis of Mantua and was educated at the city's famous humanist school, La Giocosa (see Volume 4, page 59). There he learned not only subjects such as Latin and mathematics, but also humanist virtues such as moderation and self-restraint. Writers of the time often contrasted Federigo's even temper with the fiery temper of his enemy, Sigismondo Malatesta.

Federigo was proud of both his education and his military skill. A portrait by Pedro Berruguete (shown right) emphasizes both aspects of Federigo's achievements. He is wearing armor, covered with the velvet and ermine robes of a statesman, and is reading a book. Artists portrayed Federigo only from his left side because the right side of his face had been disfigured by an accident when he was a young man. He had lost his right eye and the bridge of his nose while taking part in a joust.

Right: **Portrait of Federigo da Montefeltro and his Son Guidobaldo** *painted by Pedro Berruguete in about 1476.*

powerful Malatesta family who ruled Rimini, a city on the coast some 30 miles north of Urbino. The rivalry between the Montefeltro and Malatesta families was to continue through much of the 15th century.

Antonio's son Guidantonio had two sons: Oddantonio (1427–1444) and Federigo. In 1443 the 16-year-old Oddantonio succeeded his father as count and soon afterward was made a duke by the pope. Although Federigo was older than his brother, he could not succeed his father as count because he was illegitimate. However, Oddantonio did not remain duke of Urbino for very long. He imposed heavy taxes that soon caused his subjects to rise against him, and he was killed by one of the rebels.

At the time of the uprising the 22-year-old Federigo was away fighting Sigismondo Malatesta. Federigo quickly returned to Urbino and retook control. He won his subjects' loyalty by lowering taxes and by founding churches and monasteries. He also set about fortifying his territory, building some 70 castles in the Marches.

MILITARY SERVICE

Federigo earned money for his realm by hiring out his services as a condottiere, a kind of freelance military captain. In the 15th century the Italian states were often at war with one another. Instead of relying on a permanent army, the states would hire mercenaries (soldiers who would fight in anyone's army for the right money). Quite often the condottieri changed sides, especially if they were offered more money. However, Federigo was one of the more loyal condottieri, and his services were in great demand.

Federigo's most frequent employer was the pope. In 1461 Sigismondo Malatesta went to war with Pope Pius II, and the pope hired Federigo to fight for him. After two years Sigismondo was defeated, although not before Federigo had briefly changed sides. After Sigismondo's defeat the pope gave Federigo his rival's lands. In 1474 Pope Sixtus IV made Federigo a duke.

A RENAISSANCE COURT

Federigo used the vast sums he earned as a condottiere to create one of the most splendid courts in Italy, increasing his prestige in the eyes of both his subjects and other Italian princes. He employed great architects like Francesco di Giorgio Martini (1439–about 1501) to rebuild the Montefeltro palace, which was called the Palazzo Ducale ("palace of the duke").

The Palazzo Ducale is a masterpiece of Renaissance architecture. From the surrounding countryside it appeared to

---

Federigo used the vast sums he earned to create one of the most splendid courts in Italy

---

be a forbidding fortress. Inside, however, it was light, airy, and graceful, designed according to the latest ideas about architecture. Federigo also hired the services of numerous artists to decorate his palace. He admired oil paintings made by northern European

artists and was the only Italian Renaissance ruler to appoint a Flemish painter—Joos van Gent—as his court artist. The most celebrated painter to work at Urbino, however, was Piero della Francesca (about 1415–1492). Piero's clear, harmonious paintings were a perfect match for Federigo's cool, calm temperament.

URBINO IN DECLINE

Urbino continued to flourish after Federigo's death in 1482. His son, Guidobaldo (1472–1508), died childless and was the last Montefeltro duke. Guidobaldo's successor was his nephew and adopted son, Francesco Maria della Rovere (1490–1538). Della Rovere's court was famous for its elegance and sophistication. In his book *The Courtier* Baldassare Castiglione (1478–1529) portrayed Rovere's court at Urbino as a kind of ideal society. Although the Rovere dukes extended the duchy's lands, they lacked the energy and brilliance of the Montefeltros. Eventually the Rovere dukes moved their capital to Pesaro, and Urbino lost its importance.

Above: Federigo da Montefeltro's **studiolo,** *or "small study," in the Palazzo Ducale. It is decorated with elaborate pictures made from tiny pieces of inlaid wood using a technique called "intarsia." These pictures are some of the finest examples of intarsia work made in the Renaissance.*

SEE ALSO

- ♦ Courts and Court Culture
- ♦ Decorative Arts
- ♦ Gonzaga Family
- ♦ Piero della Francesca
- ♦ Sforza Family

Utopias

One of the most important works of Renaissance humanism was a book called *Utopia,* (1516) by the English statesman Thomas More (1477–1535). In the book More found a clever way to criticize social inequality and corruption in English society. He compared England with an imaginary island called Utopia where there was no money, and all property was shared. He made up the name "utopia" by combining two Greek words, *ou* (meaning not) and *topos* (place), so it literally means "no place." Utopia soon came to mean a fantastical, ideal community. After More's book was published, this literary device became popular among other humanist writers.

Above: An illustration from the Book of the City of Ladies, *by Christine de Pisan (1364–1430), which was published in 1405, more than 100 years before More's* Utopia. *The book describes an ideal city in which women received a good education and made many contributions to the arts and culture.*

Like many other writers, More was inspired by explorers' accounts of the New World, such as Amerigo Vespucci's *Four Voyages* (1507). In *Utopia* a traveler called Raphael Hythloday (Greek for "talker of nonsense") finds the island of Utopia during his travels with Vespucci. He discovers that the island is pagan and is governed entirely by reason, which was intended by More to be a telling comment on the corruption of the Christian Renaissance states, all of which were governed by rulers eager for power and wealth.

The writers of utopian literature also drew inspiration from classical writers. The ancient Greek philosopher Plato described a perfect society in his *Republic* (written around 350 B.C.). Plato's society was ruled by philosophers (thinkers) and had a system of state education and shared property—ideas that were popular in utopian literature of the Renaissance.

EDUCATION

Like Plato's *Republic,* most utopias were founded on a well-organized education system. In *La Città del Sole* ("The City of the Sun," 1602) the Italian thinker Tommaso Campanella railed against the stale book learning in Europe, calling it "servile book labor and memory work." His utopian city was, like More's Utopia, governed by reason. Each citizen worked for the good of others in return for his or her reasonable needs. Private property and poverty were abolished. The citizens were highly educated and valued scientific discovery and invention, and had even invented flying machines. However, an educated population came at a high price; all children were taken from their mothers at the age of two and placed in a state education system. Like other utopists, Campanella delighted in describing the benefits to the state of harsh practices like this.

SCIENTIFIC IDEAS

Campanella was fascinated by science and was a friend of Galileo's. He was persecuted for his radical ideas and wrote *La Città del Sole* while imprisoned by the Spanish Inquisition. In 1624 the English writer Francis Bacon's *New Atlantis* also described a utopia in which scientific discovery—knowledge of the "secret motions of things"—was the purpose of society.

Most utopias were intended to make the reader rethink the values of the world in which they lived. So they included quirky details as satire or to illustrate a point. More described how the citizens of Utopia, in doing away with money, had also swept away the human desire for luxury and so used gold only to make chamber pots.

Above: A 16th-century illustration of Thomas More's imaginary island Utopia, showing its many towns.

THE UTOPIAN CITY

Utopias ranged from small communities to complex cities or states. More's Utopia had 54 large towns, all with good supplies of piped fresh water. Ludovico Agostini in his *Repubblica Immaginaria* ("Imaginary Republic," 1585–1590) put the rich and poor together, living in the same streets. He had seen that in the real world the poor lived in disease-ridden slums, while the rich lived farther out in the hills around the towns.

In his book *I Mondi* ("The Worlds," 1552) Anton Francesco Doni described a circular city with one hundred streets leading out from the central square. Each street was devoted to one craft, and all the citizens lived in simple, identical houses and ate from communal kitchens. The idea of encouraging social harmony through city planning was popular in the Renaissance—Leonardo da Vinci made many sketches for such a city. The star-shaped town of Palmanova near Venice was actually built to fulfill this purpose.

SEE ALSO

- Christine de Pisan
- Humanism
- Leonardo da Vinci
- More, Thomas

Vasari

Giorgio Vasari (1511–1574) was an Italian painter, architect, and writer who did more than anyone else to promote the idea of an artistic renaissance (rebirth) in Italy during the 15th and 16th centuries. He made an enormous number of paintings and designed many buildings, but he is best known for his book *Lives of the Artists* (1550). The information and ideas it contains have shaped the way that all later scholars have looked at Renaissance art.

Vasari was born in 1511 in Arezzo, a town in Tuscany under the rule of Florence. His father was a potter (the name Vasari comes from *vasaio*, the Italian for "potter"), and Vasari soon proved a gifted child. After drawing lessons from the painter Luca Signorelli, to whom he was related, Vasari went to Florence to train under Michelangelo. When Michelangelo was called away to Rome, Vasari continued his training under the painter Andrea del Sarto. Vasari had great admiration for Michelangelo, and in later life the two men became friends.

In Florence Vasari soon came to the attention of the ruling Medici family and became their court painter. However, following a period of political turmoil in the 1520s and 1530s during which Duke Alessandro de Medici was assassinated, Vasari suffered a nervous breakdown. He left Florence and traveled around Italy, making many paintings and studying the work of other artists. By 1546 he was in Rome, where a powerful church-

man, Cardinal Farnese, asked him to paint a series of frescoes (paintings made on wet plaster) in the Palazzo della Cancelleria celebrating the life of Pope Paul III. It was at this time that Vasari wrote *Lives of the Artists*.

RETURN TO FLORENCE

In 1555 Vasari returned to Florence, where he once again became court artist to the Medici, who had been restored to power. He painted a series of frescoes in the Palazzo Vecchio celebrating the history of Florence and the Medici. With his Roman frescoes,

Above: Vasari was in his fifties and at the height of his success when he painted this **Self-Portrait** *in about 1566. He shows himself, pen in hand, wearing fashionable black robes with a grand gold chain around his neck.*

Left: The Great Council Chamber in the Palazzo Vecchio, Florence, decorated with frescoes painted by Vasari and his pupils in 1568. The large scale of the decorative scheme and its rapid execution—in just a year—are typical features of Vasari's work.

they are his best-known paintings. By now one of the most highly regarded artists in Italy, Vasari founded the Accademia del Disegno ("Academy of Design") to train young artists. It was the first art school of the time.

As well as painting, Vasari also worked as an architect. His buildings in Florence include the Uffizi (1560)—originally built as government offices and now a famous art gallery—and a tomb for Michelangelo in the church of Santa Croce. He also designed the Palazzo dei Cavalieri in Pisa and the Loggie in Arezzo. Vasari enjoyed lavish rewards for his work, including houses, offices, and favors, and he died a highly regarded artist in 1574.

LIVES OF THE ARTISTS

According to Vasari, the idea for his book on the history of Italian Renaissance art came about at a dinner in Rome, when Cardinal Farnese asked him to assemble a "catalog of artists and their works, listed in chronological order." Vasari wrote up the notes he had made during his travels and published the *Lives of the Most Eminent Italian Painters, Sculptors, and Architects* (now known as *Lives of the Artists*) in 1550. A bestseller on publication, it was enlarged in 1568. It is now the primary source of information on the artists of the Italian Renaissance.

Vasari's book includes biographies of around 160 artists. Although there are many inaccuracies, since Vasari often made up facts where information was scarce, it was the first thorough record of 15th- and 16th-century Italian art. Vasari developed the idea of an artistic renaissance that other artists and scholars of the time had begun to write about. He argued that the arts had deteriorated since the decline of ancient Rome, before being reborn around 1250 in the paintings of Cimabue and Giotto. Artistic expression then progressed through the 15th century to reach the great achievements of Leonardo da Vinci, Raphael, and Michelangelo. Michelangelo was the only living artist featured in the original edition; Vasari believed that he had brought art to a state of perfection.

SEE ALSO

- Alberti
- Classicism
- Florence
- Ghiberti
- Giotto
- Gothic Art
- Leonardo da Vinci
- Medici Family
- Michelangelo
- Painting
- Raphael
- Sculpture
- Theories of Art and Architecture

Vatican

The Vatican is the smallest independent state in the world. It covers an area of about 0.2 square miles (0.5 sq. km) on the west bank of the Tiber River in Rome. Most of its land is occupied by the great church of Saint Peter's and the Vatican Palace, a vast complex of buildings that became the official home of the popes in the late 14th century. By the 15th and 16th centuries the Vatican was the most important cultural center in Italy. The popes assembled a huge library and collection of ancient sculptures, and attracted the leading artists of the day to work there.

The Vatican is named after the Mons Vaticanus ("Vatican Mount"), one of the seven hills on which ancient Rome was built. The first church of Saint Peter's was built there in the fourth century A.D., with a bishop's palace nearby. The pope did not live in the Vatican until 1377, when Pope Gregory XI returned from Avignon in France, where the popes had been based for almost 70 years during a period of political conflict and religious controversy known as the Babylonian Captivity. During the popes' absence their traditional home in Rome, the Lateran Palace, had been badly damaged. So Pope Gregory decided to move to the Vatican, which had the added advantage of being next to the fortress of Castel Sant'Angelo should the popes ever need to take refuge in times of unrest.

From this time onward the Vatican became the official home of the popes. It was from there that they ruled the

Left: A view over the Vatican from the dome of Saint Peter's. The many buildings that now make up the palace complex were built over a period of 600 years, between the 13th and 19th centuries.

time the walls had been decorated with a series of frescoes (paintings made on wet, or "fresh," plaster) by some of the most famous Italian painters of the time, including Sandro Botticelli and Pietro Perugino. Their frescoes, however, were soon overshadowed by the paintings that Pope Julius II ordered from Michelangelo (see Volume 7, pages 4–9). From 1508 to 1512 Michelangelo painted the ceiling of the chapel with scenes from the Old Testament, which were hailed as masterpieces, while on the altar wall he painted *The Last Judgment* (1536–1541), which had a more mixed reception.

RAPHAEL AND BRAMANTE

While Michelangelo was painting the Sistine ceiling, Raphael was working nearby on frescoes to decorate four rooms in the Vatican Palace known as the *Stanze* (Italian for "rooms"). The first of these rooms, the Stanza della Segnatura, was Julius's study. Raphael decorated it with frescoes that dealt with the relationship between ancient Greek philosophy and the Christian religion. One of these frescoes, *The School of Athens,* is his best-known work (see Volume 8, page 60).

Julius II also employed the leading architect of the day, Donato Bramante, on both the rebuilding of Saint Peter's and new work at the Vatican Palace. In the Vatican Bramante designed an enormous courtyard (begun 1505) in which to display the great papal collection of classical sculpture. After Bramante's death a succession of artists took charge of Saint Peter's, including Raphael and Michelangelo.

Among the buildings added to the Vatican later in the Renaissance is the Pauline Chapel. It was begun in 1540 for Pope Paul III and is decorated with the last frescoes Michelangelo painted.

Above: The richly decorated Vatican Library. Pope Nicholas V founded the library in 1450, and it soon became one of the most comprehensive collections of books assembled in the Renaissance.

Papal States, the vast territories that they owned in central Italy. The Papal States continued to exist until the creation of modern Italy in 1870. Even then the popes were allowed to govern the Vatican, which is still technically an independent state today.

A PALACE FIT FOR THE POPE

Various popes who succeeded Gregory XI added substantially to the buildings in the Vatican, but it was not until 1450 that Pope Nicholas V began a palace that was an appropriately magnificent home for the head of the Roman Catholic church. The history of the building and decoration of the Vatican is extremely complex because so many different popes and so many different artists were involved over a very long period of time.

Pope Sixtus IV commissioned the most famous building in the Vatican— the Sistine Chapel, begun in 1477. It is the main chapel of the Vatican and is where each new pope is elected by an assembly of cardinals. The Sistine Chapel was first used in 1483, by which

SEE ALSO

♦ Antiquities
♦ Bramante
♦ Julius II
♦ Michelangelo
♦ Papacy
♦ Papal States
♦ Patronage
♦ Raphael
♦ Saint Peter's, Rome

Venice

In the early Renaissance the Italian city-state of Venice was a major European power. Its enormous wealth was based on trade, with Venetian merchants dominating the eastern Mediterranean. During the 16th century, however, the power of Venice began to decline as the rise of the Ottoman Turks and the discovery of new trade routes to Asia undermined its position.

The city of Venice is made up of a large number of tiny islands located in a lagoon off the northeast coast of Italy. Although the islands were inhabited at the time of the Roman Empire, it was not until the sixth century A.D. that the islands became home to a sizable number of people. In 727 the inhabitants of the lagoon united under a single leader, called a "doge."

For much of its early history the city of Venice was officially part of the Byzantine Empire based around the city of Constantinople (present-day Istanbul). Although Venice was virtually independent, its relationship with the Byzantine Empire allowed its merchants special privileges at key ports. From the 10th century onward the city's merchants came to dominate trade with Asia. They imported goods from Asia by transporting them along overland trade routes to Byzantine ports on the eastern shore of the Mediterranean. In the following centuries they strengthened their grip on these trade routes by forcibly taking control of a number of ports and islands in the eastern Mediterranean, building up a sizable empire that included most of the Dalmatian coast and the islands of Crete and Corfu.

ALLIES AND ENEMIES

By the late 14th century Venice was a considerable power. A bitter struggle with the rival Italian port of Genoa—a struggle that had lasted over 100

Above: A view of Venice with the Piazza San Marco in the center. The Doge's Palace, the home of the doge and the republic's governing councils, can be seen to the right of the tall bell tower; behind it the domes of Saint Mark's Basilica are just visible. The white buildings to the left of the bell tower housed the republic's mint and library.

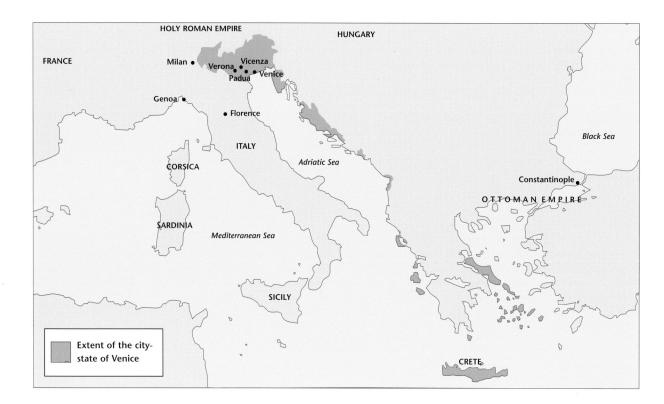

years—ended with victory for Venice at the battle of Chioggia in 1381. Venice's rulers now began to turn their attention inward and in the early 15th century concentrated on expanding the land under their control in northern Italy. By 1405 Venice had taken control of the nearby cities of Padua, Vicenza, and Verona. By 1428 it had also conquered Brescia and Bergamo. Venice now ruled a large inland region that provided both a market for its traders' goods and food for the city's population. The area became known as the Veneto.

In Italy's complex political situation city-states constantly formed and broke alliances with one another in their struggle for power. Venice's most important ally in the early 15th century was Florence, with which it combined against Milan. The situation changed in 1450, when Francesco Sforza became duke of Milan. His rise to power caused a change of allegiances, and Venice now saw Milan as an ally. In 1454 Venice signed a peace treaty with Milan, and a year later Venice, Florence, and Milan joined an alliance called the Italian League, which aimed to maintain the peace in Italy.

TRADE AND INDUSTRY

By now Venice was at the height of its power. In the mid-15th century the population of the city was around 100,000, while the surrounding land was home to a further million citizens. Venice's vast merchant fleet continued to supply Europe with large quantities of goods from Asia and the Middle East, and the city was an important center for manufacture, producing fine silk textiles and glassware.

Venice was also the site of the Arsenale, a gigantic shipyard where vessels were both made and repaired. Historians have compared the techniques used at the Arsenale to those employed on a modern factory production line. Teams of 20 men worked on the ship at each phase of its

Above: A map showing the extent of the city-state of Venice in the 15th century. Venice's trading empire in the eastern Mediterranean was under constant threat from the Ottoman Turks.

construction. Vessels in various stages of construction were towed from one area of the shipyard to another, where they were assembled and equipped with sails, ropes, and armaments, all of which were made in the Arsenale. The Arsenale employed huge numbers of workers—in the middle of the 16th century 16,000 men worked there. They enjoyed special privileges and were comparatively well paid.

Despite Venice's great wealth and increased territory, its trading empire in the eastern Mediterranean was under threat. Throughout the 15th century the power of the Ottoman Turks had been steadily increasing. In 1416 Venice had defeated the Turkish fleet at the naval battle of Gallipoli, but this had not checked the Ottomans' advance. In 1453 the Ottoman sultan Mehmed II captured Constantinople

THE VENETIAN SYSTEM OF GOVERNMENT

Compared to other Italian city-states in the Renaissance, Venice was a model of political stability. Ever since the early 12th century Venice had been a republic. The city was led by an elected leader called the doge, whose actions were controlled by a number of councils, including the Great Council, the Senate, and the Council of Ten. All matters of government were conducted in the Doge's Palace.

The Great Council was the most important of these organizations. Originally it had 45 members, but it gradually increased in size until it had more than 1,000 members. In 1297 an act was passed known as the *Serrata del Maggior Consiglio*, or "Closure of the Great Council." This act limited participation in the council to a set number of noble families.

The existence of a variety of councils and committees whose different interests balanced each other, as well as the mature age of the more influential members of government, ensured the stability of the Venetian republic. The negative side of the Venetian political system was the fact that the majority of the city's inhabitants were excluded from the political process. However, there were remarkably few revolts against the government.

Left: A painting made in the 17th century showing the doge and members of his government receiving guests. The meeting is taking place in the Sala del Collegio, one of the grandest rooms in the Doge's Palace.

and destroyed the Byzantine Empire. The Ottomans then pushed into Greece and the Balkans, threatening the Venetians' trading empire.

At first the Venetians tried to keep the Turks at bay through diplomacy. Eventually, however, the two powers clashed. The first Turkish war lasted from 1463 to 1479 and ended in defeat for Venice. The republic was forced to pay tribute to the Ottoman sultan and to give up control of the island of Negroponte. Venice suffered further losses in a second Turkish war (1499–1503), which ended when the Venetians signed another disadvantageous treaty.

DECLINING FORTUNES

The early 16th century saw a decline in Venice's fortunes. The city's growth in the previous century had alarmed many of its rivals, who in 1508 formed the League of Cambrai to limit the republic's power. Among the league's members were the most powerful rulers in Europe—Pope Julius II, King Louis XII of France, and the Holy Roman Emperor Maximilian I. The league defeated the Venetians at the battle of Agnadello in 1509, and many cities that had previously been under Venice's control joined the league. Because the league's members squabbled among themselves, Venice itself was never attacked, and many of the cities in the Veneto eventually returned to Venetian control. However, the battle of Agnadello was a turning point in Venice's fortunes. The war was extremely expensive and put an end to Venice's aggressive policy of acquiring new territories on the mainland.

NEW TRADE ROUTES

The discovery of new trade routes at the end of the 15th century also delivered a serious blow to Venice. Christopher Columbus's discovery of the Americas in 1492 presented fresh opportunities to merchants based on the Atlantic coast, particularly those from Portugal.

More damaging from a Venetian point of view was Vasco da Gama's voyage to India of 1497 to 1499. Da Gama reached India by sailing around the Cape of Good Hope, the southernmost tip of Africa. Previously goods from Asia, most importantly spices, had reached Europe via overland trade routes that crossed Asia. This arrangement favored the Venetians, with their extensive contacts in the eastern Mediterranean. The new routes allowed merchants from Portugal, Spain, and northern Europe to import goods directly by sea without dealing with the Venetians.

Below: A detail from a 17th-century map of Venice showing the city's great shipyard, the Arsenale. It shows sailing ships moving along the waterways that run within the vast complex of workshops.

ARSENAL

VENETIAN ART

As Venice grew prosperous on trade, the city became an important center for the arts. Venetian artists and craftsmen were strongly influenced by the cosmopolitan environment of the city. In the 15th and 16th centuries Venice led the way in the production of luxury glass and was also an important center for making silk fabric. In both these activities Venetian craftsmen were influenced by their contacts with the east, from where these products had been imported since the Middle Ages. Venetian painters had long been influenced by Byzantine art. In the Renaissance they were also some of the first Italian artists to embrace developments taking place in northern European painting. They started to use oil paint, began to portray holy figures in a more intimate, lifelike way, and painted detailed, realistic portraits. These developments were first seen in the work of the Bellini family—Jacopo and his two sons Gentile and Giovanni. They ran the city's leading workshop in the 15th century and trained many of the next generation of artists, including Giorgione and Titian.

Titian was the most important Venetian artist of the Renaissance. He developed a style of painting based on rich color and loose brushwork. His portraits and paintings of religious and mythological subjects were collected by some of the most powerful men in

Above: **The Assumption of the Virgin (1516–1518) by Titian. The rich colors and dramatic arrangement of this painting made Titian's name in Venice.**

Europe, and his style shaped the work of other Venetian artists, especially Jacopo Tintoretto and Paolo Veronese.

In the first half of the 16th century Italy was a battleground on which the two most powerful nations in Europe—Spain and France—fought each other for supremacy. Eventually the Spanish Hapsburg king and Holy Roman emperor Charles V proved victorious, and almost the entire peninsula became part of the Hapsburgs' vast territories. Venice was the only state to remain independent.

The city's merchants managed to adjust to the new economic conditions, and the textile industry in particular continued to thrive. The city also flourished as an artistic center and was home to such great artists as Titian, Jacopo Tintoretto, and Paolo Veronese. Although Venice never recovered its earlier power and wealth, it remained stable and relatively prosperous for the remainder of the 16th century.

Veronese

Paolo Veronese (about 1528–1588) was one of the leading painters in Venice during the second half of the 16th century. He is best known for his large, decorative frescoes (wall paintings made on wet, or "fresh," plaster), which are full of brilliant colors, stunning visual effects, and playful details.

Veronese's real name was Paolo Caliari, but he was nicknamed "Veronese" because he came from the city of Verona on the Venetian mainland. Veronese was influenced by the work of Titian, who was the leading painter in Venice, particularly his use of rich color and free handling of paint.

Veronese's paintings decorate many of Venice's palaces and churches, as well as the new country villas that were built on the mainland. In the 1560s he painted frescoes in the Villa Maser, designed by the leading architect of the time, Andrea Palladio (see Volume 8,

page 7). He also painted many pictures with religious subjects. In 1573, for example, he painted *The Last Supper* for the dining room of a Dominican monastery. In the painting Jesus and his disciples are almost lost behind a host of elegantly dressed men, servants, dwarfs, and dogs. The church court known as the Inquisition criticized the painting because it did not seem respectful enough. Veronese agreed to change the title to *The Feast in the House of Levi*, a subject in which his details would cause less offense.

Veronese painted one of his most spectacular frescoes, *The Triumph of Venice*, on a ceiling in the Doge's Palace in Venice. In the painting angels crown a magnificently dressed woman, who symbolizes Venice. Below her is a crowd of onlookers, including soldiers, priests, and beautiful women. Veronese painted the fresco in such a way that the figures seem to float above the viewer in the chamber below.

Above: **The Feast in the House of Levi,** *painted by Veronese in 1573. Veronese intended the picture to show the Last Supper of Christ; but because he included so many details of feasting and festivity, the church authorities insisted that he change the title.*

SEE ALSO

◆ Palladio
◆ Titian

Verrocchio

Today Andrea del Verrocchio (about 1435–1488) is best known as the teacher of Leonardo da Vinci (1452–1519). In the late 15th century, however, Verrocchio was celebrated as a great sculptor, and he ran the largest, busiest workshop in Florence. He was also one of the favorite artists of the powerful Medici family. They asked him to make statues and fountains for their palaces, as well as tombs and monuments for Florence's churches.

Some scholars think that Verrocchio was a pupil of Donatello (about 1386–1466), the greatest Italian sculptor of the early 15th century. The two artists' work was very different, however. Donatello's sculptures are full of passion and heroism, while Verrocchio's are refined and graceful. In this way his work looks forward to the elegant style of the 16th century known as "mannerism."

In some of his sculptures Verrocchio was clearly trying to surpass Donatello's achievements. In about 1470, for example, he made a statue of the Old Testament hero David standing over the head of the giant Goliath, whom he has just slayed; Donatello had made a similar sculpture almost 40 years before (see Volume 5, page 24). Like Donatello, Verrocchio also sculpted an equestrian monument, a large statue showing a soldier or leader on horseback. Verrocchio's monument was made in 1481–1496 to commemorate Bartolommeo Colleoni, a mercenary (a soldier whose services are for hire) who had fought for Venice. The sculpture is almost 12 ft (4m) high, making it larger than a similar monument made by Donatello to commemorate a mercenary known as Gattamelata (see Volume 3, page 30). Verrocchio's horse is full of movement and energy. He was the first artist to sculpt a horse with one leg off the ground as if it were moving, a great technical feat since the huge weight of the sculpture has to be supported by only three slender legs.

Verrocchio worked as a painter as well as a sculptor. In about 1470 he painted *The Baptism of Christ* with the assistance of the young Leonardo da Vinci. Verrocchio is said to have been so impressed by his pupil's skill that he gave up painting.

Left: Verrocchio's bronze sculpture David (1470), one of his best-known works. Verrocchio shows David as an elegant youth, standing hand on hip and holding the sword with which he has just cut off the head of the giant Goliath.

SEE ALSO

♦ Artists' Workshops
♦ Donatello
♦ Leonardo da Vinci
♦ Mannerism
♦ Sculpture

Violence

Left: A late 16th-century engraving showing a massacre and pillaging in Sens, a town in Burgundy, in April 1562 during the French Wars of Religion (1562–1598). Ordinary people often suffered at the hands of soldiers in the many wars of the Renaissance.

Although the Renaissance is best known as a time of great artistic achievement, it was also a period when violence was an everyday fact of life. There was constant warfare, and roving bands of former soldiers and bandits terrorized the countryside. People made desperate by poverty committed many violent crimes. When caught, criminals were publicly punished by violent acts such as hanging, mutilation, or flogging, and the Inquisition tortured and burned those it declared to be heretics, or people who rejected the teachings of the Catholic church.

Violence occurred at all levels of society. Many respected figures became involved in fights; Michelangelo's nose was broken as the result of a quarrel with a fellow sculptor, and the English playwright Ben Jonson killed the actor Gabriel Spencer in a tavern brawl. Faced with unruly and dangerous behavior, many town authorities tried to legislate against the carrying of arms in towns and public places; but the lack of an effective police force made laws difficult to apply.

FEUDS AND VENDETTAS

There were many feuds and vendettas, and people enlisted help from their friends and family to revenge wrongs done to them. These situations could quickly spiral out of control, creating large-scale clan warfare, such as the violent conflict between the Montagues and Capulets in Renaissance Verona, which was immortalized by William Shakespeare in his play *Romeo and Juliet*. Even in cultural centers such as Florence conflict between the followers of rival nobles could often make the streets dangerous places.

Much violence was taken for granted. Pastimes such as bullbaiting, cockfighting, and stoning dogs and cats were popular. Public executions, often prolonged by tortures and maiming, drew large crowds. Traitors' heads were impaled on spikes on city walls, and convicted criminals' bodies hung from gibbets at crossroads.

YOUNG PEOPLE

Violence was seen as a young person's problem—half the European population was under 20. Many boys —apprentices, students, soldiers— lived away from their parents from a very young age and held little respect for authority. Gangs of young men were some of the main perpetrators of violence. Sometimes this violence was fueled by a sense of injustice; the gangs of apprentices that terrorized many cities were often enraged by their limited job prospects and sense of exclusion at a time when many guilds would not admit new members.

The many wars of the Renaissance also created a large pool of disaffected, and often unpaid, soldiers who were ruthless, undernourished, and used to violence. They turned on the population of the places they passed through. In the Schmalkaldic War of 1546 the atrocities of Charles V's Spanish troops against the civilian population included attacking women and girls and torturing men to reveal where they had hidden their money.

Above: A 16th-century painting showing an armed attack in the woods. Travelers were always at risk from bandits and robbers who roamed the woods and highways waiting to prey on innocent victims.

VANDALISM

The passions aroused by the Reformation led to widespread acts of desecration and violence. Protestants rejected the paintings, images, and decoration of Catholic churches in favor of plain, unadorned places of worship, and this was frequently taken to extremes. Some desecrations of Catholic churches were simply acts of vandalism by people who resented the wealth of the church and felt oppressed by its authority. Erasmus described an orgy of destruction in Basel in 1529, commenting that "not a statue had been left in the churches, in porches, on façades, or in the monasteries. Everything frescoed is lost under coats of whitewash. Whatever would burn has been thrown into the pyre."

The most notorious act of vandalism in the Renaissance was the sack of Rome in 1527 by the troops of the Holy Roman emperor Charles V. For eight days the soldiers pillaged the city, destroying countless works of art, and forcing Pope Clement VII to take refuge in Castel Sant' Angelo. One soldier even scratched "Martin Luther" on Raphael's fresco *The Triumph of the Sacrament* in the Vatican.

SEE ALSO

♦ Crime and Punishment
♦ Inquisition
♦ Justice and the Law
♦ Poverty
♦ Rome

Left: A 16th-century painting showing the defeat of the Ottomans at the naval battle of Lepanto in 1571. The Ottomans were trying to expand into the eastern Mediterranean and had invaded Cyprus, but were defeated by allied Christian forces. The Europeans saw this as a great victory, and many pictures were painted to commemorate it.

Warfare

The Renaissance was a period of great artistic advance and achievement. However, it was also a period of bloody warfare all over Europe, Asia, and the Middle East. On its borders Europe was constantly threatened by the expanding Ottoman Empire. Internally, the religious split caused by the Reformation worsened the tensions and rivalries between states, cities, and rulers that often spilled over into war.

The key to warfare over much of the world was the expansion of Islamic empires. In the late 14th century Tamerlane (also known as Timur) led his Mongol armies across Central Asia into Persia (present-day Iran), India, and the Middle East. He used speed to unsettle his enemies and was completely ruthless. When he sacked Delhi in 1398, for example, he slaughtered the inhabitants and made great pyramids of human heads. His greatest victory came at Ankara in 1402, when he defeated the armies of the Ottoman Empire and captured their sultan Bayezid. After Tamerlane's death in 1405, however, his empire fell apart. Another Mongol leader, Babur, conquered north India after a great victory at Panipat in 1526 and established the Mogul Empire. He carried on a series of wars, especially against Hindu Indian kingdoms.

TECHNOLOGY

The battlefield of 1600 was very unlike that of 1400. The most important change was the widespread use of gunpowder weapons. At the battle of Agincourt in 1415 there were no hand-held gunpowder weapons, but by 1600 about two-thirds of all infantrymen carried one. It would probably be an arquebus or a matchlock, so called because the gunpowder was ignited by a length of burning cord known as the match. These weapons were unwieldy and unreliable, but they changed the face of the battlefield. The remainder of an infantry force would be armed with pikes to ward off enemy cavalry while the soldiers armed with arquebuses reloaded. Many cavalry carried guns in addition to lances and swords. Guns for use on horseback were usually firelocks, in which a circular mechanism struck flint against steel to create a spark, and they were shorter than infantry weapons so they could be fired with one hand.

Since guns could penetrate all but the thickest plate armor, the mounted knight of the late Middle Ages, encased in armor from head to toe, became a thing of the past, although many soldiers still wore helmets, and some had breastplates.

Below: A 16th-century tapestry of the battle of Pavia, 1525, when Francis I of France was defeated by the emperor Charles V.

In the Middle East three Islamic empires came into conflict: Persia, the Ottomans, and the Mamluks, a warrior caste that had taken over Egypt in the 13th century. The Mamluks were particularly renowned as cavalry soldiers and extended their power over the Arabian peninsula and along the coast of North Africa. However, they were defeated by Ottoman forces, which entered Cairo in 1517.

OTTOMAN EMPIRE

The Ottoman forces that defeated the Mamluks were a formidable army. European history in the Renaissance period was defined by the threat from the Ottomans. They made their first important European conquest in 1361, when they took Adrianople (present-day Erdine) in Thrace. Constantinople fell in 1453; and in 1529 the Ottomans advanced as far as Vienna in Austria, which they besieged unsuccessfully.

There was a great rivalry between the Ottomans and Venice in the Mediterranean. The Ottomans conquered several Venetian possessions before being defeated by Christian forces at the battle of Lepanto in 1571. Had the Ottoman sultans not also been engaged in wars against Persia to the east, they would probably have made greater conquests in Europe.

In facing the wealthy, unified Ottoman state, European forces were often at a disadvantage. They were not unified, and no single state could

Above: A 16th-century book illustration of French artillery, showing a mortar and two cannons. The development of mobile cannons in the Renaissance period completely changed the nature of warfare.

match Ottoman resources. The Ottoman victory over Hungary at Mohacs in 1526 was made easier because German princes did not agree to send help to the Hungarians until it was too late, while the French king Francis I secretly proposed an alliance to the Ottoman sultan as a way of weakening his enemy, the Hapsburg emperor Charles V.

EUROPEAN WARS

Within Europe the antagonism between states, cities, and spiritual leaders provided fertile ground for warfare. France and England were involved in a long struggle, known as the Hundred Years' War, from the 14th century until the French victory of Castillon in 1453. Henry V of England won a great victory at Agincourt in 1415, but the French managed to recover lost ground, partly due to the heroism of Joan of Arc. After the war ended, England was plunged into a civil war known as the Wars of the Roses, while France recovered its strength and gradually asserted itself over the powerful duchy of Burgundy.

During the 15th century there was frequent warfare in Italy between city-states such as Milan, Venice, Genoa, and Florence. Most of the fighting on land was conducted by mercenary armies, which were concerned to minimize casualties. This rather gentlemanly form of war came to an abrupt end when Charles VIII of France invaded Italy in 1494. He was opposed by a "Holy League" of Venice, Milan, Spain, the pope, and the Holy Roman emperor, and warfare broke out every few years in Italy for the next 35 years. The treaty of Cambrai in 1529 between Charles V and Francis I brought this particular phase of European war to a close.

There was frequent warfare in Italy between the various city-states

---

The wars in Italy saw several important developments in the nature of warfare. Mobile cannons, which were able to support an army in the field or blow apart fortifications, became indispensable. In addition, infantry rather than cavalry became the core of an army. Some of these infantry harked back to an earlier period of warfare. Swiss pikemen, for example, were employed as mercenaries and sometimes took the field on their own behalf. However, their deep formations proved vulnerable to artillery fire and were exposed at the battle of Marignano in 1515. The future lay with Spanish infantrymen, organized in units known as *tercios*. They used various weapons, from hand-held gunpowder weapons to pikes and swords, and were flexible enough to adapt to different requirements in battle.

RELIGIOUS WARS

A new source of conflict emerged with the split in the church caused by the Reformation of the 16th century. The earliest Protestant rulers were German princes who saw the new religion of Lutheranism as a chance to challenge the Holy Roman emperor and increase their own independence. They formed the Schmalkaldic League in 1531, a military alliance against the Catholic Hapsburg emperor. He was forced to concede them rights to determine the religion of their own lands, since he feared they would otherwise ally themselves with the Hapsburgs' enemy, France. Within France itself, however, there was bitter conflict between Catholics and French Protestants (known as Huguenots). The French Wars of Religion broke out in 1562 and continued until the Huguenot Henry of Navarre took the throne, converted to Catholicism, and issued the Edict of Nantes, granting tolerance to the Huguenots in 1598.

The Dutch revolted against their Catholic ruler, Philip II of Spain, in 1566. The loss of traditional freedoms and religious persecution—the inhabitants of the northern areas were often Protestant—played a key role in their struggle. The fighting dragged on

Below: A 16th-century painted panel showing the Spanish conqueror Hernán Cortés marching into the Aztec capital city of Tenochtitlan in Mexico in 1521. Cortés captured the city with only a few hundred Spanish soldiers and Native American allies.

ARTISTS AND WAR

War and political upheaval were facts of life for Renaissance artists, and they frequently became involved in a way that would be unusual today. Leonardo da Vinci, for example, worked for the duke of Milan as a military engineer. Sandro Botticelli was involved in the religious revolution in Florence led by the monk Savonarola and may have destroyed some of his own paintings because he came to believe they represented evil. Toward the end of the Renaissance period the Flemish painter Rubens was employed on diplomatic duties by the Spanish monarchy.

Artists became involved in war and politics because they needed wealthy and important individuals to commission their works of art. Such individuals were likely to be involved in political struggles in a warlike age, and so the artists who worked for them naturally became involved as well.

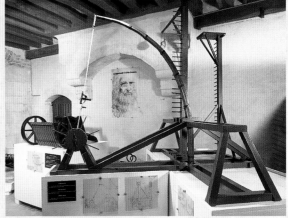

Above: Modern models of a catapult (front) and machine gun (rear) designed by Leonardo da Vinci.

through the rest of the century, and the northern provinces eventually achieved their independence in 1648.

The Dutch were given help against Spain by England, so Philip II decided to invade England in the 1580s. He also had a wider religious ambition to bring

---

In the 1550s Ivan the Terrible took Mongol strongholds and removed the Mongol threat forever

---

Protestant England back to the Catholic church. But Philip abandoned his invasion attempts after the defeat of his great Armada of warships in 1588.

Philip had also hoped to end English attacks on Spain's overseas empire. Although the period of the Renaissance had seen Europe under great pressure from the Ottomans in the southeast, by the late 16th century Europe had become an expansionist continent in other directions. In eastern Europe Russian, Polish, and Lithuanian forces were able to defeat the Mongols who had regularly raided them from the steppes and demanded tribute. In the 1550s the Russian czar Ivan the Terrible took the Mongol strongholds of Kazan and Astrakhan, removing the Mongol threat forever.

The greatest European expansion was in the Americas. The Spanish defeated the empire of the Aztecs in the 1520s and that of the Incas in the 1530s with a combination of surprise, courage, better weapons, and the fact that the local peoples died from European diseases. In Asia, too, the Portuguese defeated local rulers to establish a set of trading posts in the Indian Ocean. Such conquests set a pattern that was to be repeated many times in the following two centuries as various European powers conquered and colonized many areas of the globe.

Wars of Religion

The Reformation of the 16th century and the setting up of reformed Protestant churches led to many outbreaks of civil unrest. While some rulers welcomed the new churches and made Protestantism their official religion, others remained staunchly committed to the Catholic church and persecuted anyone who dared to profess the new faith. Nowhere were these tensions more pronounced than in France, where religious conflict led to almost 40 years of bitter civil war known as the Wars of Religion.

By the mid-16th century France was divided into the two main religious groups—Catholics and Protestants, who were known as Huguenots. The Huguenots were particularly powerful in the south and west. On one hand the Catholics, who formed the majority of French citizens, felt threatened by the new doctrines of the Protestants. On the other the Huguenots were angry that they were denied basic rights, such as freedom to worship. Although they were relatively small in number, the Huguenots had considerable influence. Many were well-off merchants and craftsmen, and some came from the nobility. In the end the friction between the Catholics and Huguenots broke out into a series of bloody conflicts that lasted from 1562 to 1598.

After the death of the French king Henry II in 1559 tension between the two sides increased. The crown passed successively to Henry's young sons,

Left: A 16th-century engraving of the battle of Dreux (December 1562), one of the first battles fought in the French Wars of Religion. The leaders of both sides were killed in the battle, and the warring Catholics and Huguenots signed the Peace of Amboise in March 1563. But the truce was short-lived, and fighting soon broke out again.

Francis II (1544–1560), Charles IX (1550–1574), and Henry III (1551–1589). Each was dominated by their mother, Catherine de Medici (1519–1589). Although she was Catholic, Catherine's main concern was to maintain peace and stability, so she tried to reach a compromise with the Huguenots. From 1562 the Huguenots were allowed to hold church services away from town centers. Catherine also arranged for her daughter Margaret to marry a Huguenot noble, Henry of Navarre, who was next in line to the throne after Catherine's four sons.

A MASSACRE SPARKS CIVIL WAR

These concessions failed to prevent war. The massacre of a Protestant congregation at the town of Vassey in March 1562 led to the first outbreak of full-scale war, which lasted for a year and ended with an uneasy truce. Conflict broke out once more until 1570, when the Peace of Saint Germain-en-Laye granted a degree of tolerance to the Huguenots. Then in 1572 thousands of Huguenots were killed in what came to be known as the

---

Throughout the wars both sides committed terrible atrocities

Saint Bartholomew's Day Massacre (see box). Outraged by the slaughter, the Huguenots became more determined than ever to stand up for their rights. They also no longer felt bound to keep to the Calvinist principle of obedience to royal authority. Civil war continued on and off for the next 12 years. Throughout the wars both sides committed terrible atrocities. One Huguenot commander is said to have made himself a necklace out of the ears

Right: A 17th-century painting of Henry IV of France besieging Paris in the early 1590s. Henry became king of France in 1589 but had to fight the Catholic League, which would not accept a Protestant king. In the end Henry converted to Catholicism in 1593 and entered a hostile Paris in 1594. He finally established peace in 1598 with the Edict of Nantes.

THE SAINT BARTHOLOMEW'S DAY MASSACRE

The worst atrocity of the French Wars of Religion was the Saint Bartholomew's Day Massacre, in which thousands of Protestant Huguenots were killed by Catholics. The massacre happened during celebrations of the marriage of Catherine de Medici's daughter Margaret to the Protestant noble Henry of Navarre in Paris in August 1572. Many Huguenots had gathered in Paris for the wedding. An assassin tried to kill a leading Huguenot named Admiral de Coligny, seemingly under the orders of Catherine herself and the powerful Catholic Guise family. The Huguenots were outraged by the attempted murder and went to the king, Catherine's young son Charles IX, to demand that he bring those responsible for the attempted crime to justice.

Catherine managed to convince Charles that the Protestants were planning to kill him, so he agreed to launch a strike against the leading Huguenots first. On August 24, Saint Bartholomew's Day, the king's soldiers set out to kill their Huguenot victims—though Henry of Navarre was spared. Mobs

of Catholic Parisians joined in the massacre, roaming the streets and hunting down the Protestants. By evening the Seine River was red with blood. As news of the Paris killings spread, Protestants were massacred all across France. Nobody knows exactly how many Huguenots died, but estimates vary from 20,000 to 70,000 people.

Above: A contemporary painting of the massacre of Protestants in Paris in 1572.

of Catholic priests. Both sides were guilty of badly maltreating prisoners, sometimes even killing them.

WAR OF THE THREE HENRYS

In 1584 Henry III's younger brother died; and because the king was childless, Henry of Navarre became heir to the throne. Frightened by the prospect of a Protestant king, the Catholics, led by Henry, duke of Guise, formed a Catholic League and forced the king to revoke past agreements granting tolerance to the Huguenots. The Huguenots rose in protest, and a new war, the War of the Three Henrys (1585–1589), broke out. In 1589 Henry III was assassinated by a fanatical priest, and Henry of Navarre became king. The civil war continued because much of the country did not accept the new monarch, including Paris. Spain also sent an invasion force against the Huguenots. Henry IV realized that a Protestant king would never be accepted, so in 1593 he converted to Catholicism. With charm, threats, and money he then proceeded to win over many Catholics to his side. But the more extreme Catholics and Protestants remained hostile toward him.

In 1598 Henry managed to end the Wars of Religion with the proclamation of the Edict of Nantes. This edict granted the Huguenots the freedom to worship and full civic rights.

SEE ALSO

♦ Calvin
♦ France
♦ Protestantism
♦ Reformation

Wealth

The Renaissance period saw a dramatic change in the ownership of wealth. In the Middle Ages only kings, the nobility, and the church were rich. However, the great increase in trade in the 15th and 16th centuries, coupled with a huge influx of gold and silver from the New World, meant that a large number of merchants and bankers became extremely prosperous. These newly rich people were eager to show off their wealth. They paid for imposing palaces, villas, churches, libraries, statues, and paintings, and bought expensive clothes and jewelry to show the world how rich and powerful they were. To a great extent the artistic and cultural achievements of the Renaissance were a result of this newly acquired wealth.

Traditionally wealth was associated with land ownership and was largely the preserve of the nobility. This situation began to change in the 12th century. Towns became centers for trade and, increasingly, for wealth. The process was speeded up by the Black Death, which killed around one-third of Europe's population in the 14th century. The resulting shortage of workers meant that wages rose, and so farming became more expensive. As landowners tried to reduce their costs, jobless peasants flocked to the towns. Although the population of Europe fell dramatically between 1300 and 1500, during the same period the number of towns with more than 10,000 inhabitants increased from 125 to 154.

Above: A 16th-century portrait of a noblewoman. She is wearing a gown and hat made of expensive red velvet decorated with gold thread and jewels, and has a tippet (cape) of fur around her shoulders. This display of rich clothing and jewelry was intended to show her wealth and social status.

Such changes undermined the traditional wealth of the nobility. In the flourishing urban centers merchants grew wealthy from trade. As trade increased, merchants began to act as moneylenders and bankers to nobles, emerging as a new rich and powerful social group. Banking families such as the Fuggers of Augsburg and the Medici of Florence financed the wars and expensive lifestyles of nobles and even monarchs. In the late Renaissance, for example, the Spanish crown was the biggest single debtor in Europe, dependent on loans from wealthy banking families.

Wealth was redistributed even further if nobles were unable to repay their loans. Instead of handing over money, they transferred their land to their creditors. In this way the Fugger banking family gained a virtual monopoly (exclusive control) of the European silver mining industry, while the Medici family gained control of Italy's supplies of alum, an essential product in the dyeing process.

PATRONS OF THE ARTS

Just as the nature of the wealthy changed, so did attitudes toward wealth. Rich individuals and institutions wanted to display their prestige by buying luxury goods and accumulating possessions. They competed to commission the best artists and architects, and then specified that artists use expensive colors, such as ultramarine, which was ground from the semiprecious stone lapis lazuli.

People often commissioned portraits of themselves wearing expensive fabrics, such as damask, or surrounded by rich belongings. Towns and guilds also spent money lavishly on churches, monuments and memorials, and guildhalls. The Catholic church traditionally condemned such obvious displays of wealth, so rich citizens also spent lavishly on hospitals and other good works or left money for charitable uses. Such charity, however, also served to advertise the donor's prestige and was in some ways another kind of vanity.

However wealthy people became, there were limits to what their money could buy. Even the wealthiest citizens did not live comfortably by today's standards. Stone houses were large but cold and drafty, and offered little privacy. Although the rich could buy luxurious foods such as sugar and pepper, and plates and forks to eat with, the food they ate was distinguished more by quantity—particularly of meat—than by quality. Lack of proper sanitation and clean drinking water affected the rich as well as the poor, and no amount of wealth could protect its owner against disease.

Left: A detail from a painting by Jan Bruegel the Elder (1568–1625) showing a table laden with luxurious gold and silver ware. Wealthy merchants often filled their houses with expensive items to enhance their prestige.

Women

In the 15th and 16th centuries most European women were peasants. The rest belonged to the artisan (craftspeople) social group or were born into wealthy merchant families, the nobility, or the monarchy. Whatever social group they came from, most women were expected to stay at home, bear children, and run their household. A very few privileged women received an education, and some outstanding women excelled as poets, writers, painters, or religious reformers. The Renaissance also saw a number of powerful and effective women rulers.

The life of a peasant woman was unrelenting drudgery from dawn to dusk. She would care for her children, prepare the family's food, carry water from the stream or well, make the family's clothes, do the laundry, look after any animals the family owned, such as a cow, pig, or chickens, tend the vegetable patch, and preserve food for winter. At especially busy times of the farming year, such as harvest, she was also expected to help out in the fields.

A woman of the artisan group might work alongside her menfolk, sharing their skills, such as those of a blacksmith or cobbler. Or she might have a skill of her own, such as lacemaking, spinning, or weaving, which she could carry out in her own home. Daughters of peasant and artisan families often went out to work at a very early age as servants in richer households. Wealthy women and

Left: A detail from a 16th-century painting by Jan Bruegel the Elder showing daily life in the countryside. Among the tasks the peasant women are doing are making butter in a large churn (left), fetching water, preparing a meal, looking after children, and bringing home pails of milk.

Above: A 15th-century book illustration showing a group of noble-women engaged in making cloth for their household. The wool is carded (center), then spun into thread (left), and finally woven into cloth on a loom (rear).

traveling players, or of a gipsy band, or be camp followers—the body of women that traveled with an army as wives, mistresses, laundresses, cooks, and nurses.

MARRIAGE

The aim and destiny of most women was to marry. Marriage among poorer people was an economic necessity. Husband and wife often worked alongside each other, and the children of the marriage were expected to contribute to the family's work and income from a very early age. If the parents lived into old age, the children were expected to support them. If a wife died from disease or in childbirth, the husband would remarry as soon as possible to make the family unit complete again.

High-ranking women frequently had little choice when it came to marriage. Prominent families saw marriage as a way of forging diplomatic and territorial alliances. For example, Lucrezia Borgia (1480–1519), a member of one of the most powerful families in Italy, was married three times by the time she was 22 in a succession of dynastic alliances dictated by her father, Pope Alexander VI, and brother, Cesare Borgia.

noblewomen were responsible for running their households, ordering and buying food, managing the servants and the household accounts, and caring for the children.

Most women remained in the same locality throughout their lives. They might travel the short distance from their village to market or to visit relatives in a nearby town, but they rarely ventured farther afield. Travel was dangerous and expensive, and the few adventurous female travelers belonged to a colorful minority. They might be members of a troupe of

CHILDBEARING

Most women's lives were dominated by childbearing—on average, women gave birth to six or seven children. The chances of dying in childbirth were high—about five women died for every 100 births. This was partly because people did not understand the importance of cleanliness—bedclothes were dirty, the midwives' hands were unwashed, and infection was common. Many children died in infancy—a quarter to a third of all children died in

Above: A painting of the marriage of Eleonora of Toledo and Cosimo de Medici in 1539.

recover from the birth, it could also distance her from her children.

Women who did not marry or who were widowed were in a precarious position both socially and financially—any inheritance would pass directly to male family members. The lucky ones could expect to be cared for by their male relatives, but many were dependent on charity. Some unmarried women took refuge in convents, passing the rest of their lives in prayer and contemplation—but after the Reformation this was only possible in Catholic countries. Many unfortunate women had to survive as best they could and were forced to become servants, prostitutes, or beggars.

WITCH HUNTS

In the 16th and 17th centuries a witch-hunting craze swept through Europe in which an estimated 100,000 people died. Around 80 percent of the victims were women. It is not clear why so many women were persecuted. Many of the victims were older widows or unmarried women. These women, who often lived alone, were regarded with suspicion, which all too easily turned to hysterical fear. When livestock, crops,

their first year, and just over half survived to the age of 10. It was fashionable for women who could afford it to give their children to wet nurses to breast-feed them. While this gave the mother the opportunity to

THE URSULINE ORDER

Women who did not marry often made religion the focus of their lives and dedicated themselves to prayer. Some religious women, such as Angela Merici, chose a more dynamic path. Merici was born in 1474 in Venice and was orphaned at age 10. She dedicated herself to charitable work after being influenced by the work of nuns and Franciscans. In 1506 she had a vision in which she was promised that she would found "a society of virgins" before she died.

In 1531 Merici recruited a dozen young women as teachers, and in 1535 she founded the Company of

Saint Ursula (the Ursulines) in Brescia, north Italy. She believed nuns should be socially useful and proposed the idea that the religious sisters should live and work within the community. The sisters made no formal vows, although they had to adhere to the strict principles of poverty, chastity, and obedience. They lived in their own homes and worked in their own locality. The Ursuline Order was the first institution dedicated to the education of girls. It became the greatest women's teaching order and provided many educational opportunities for women.

or people suffered from some unexplained disease, such women were often accused of having caused the problem by witchcraft.

WOMEN AND EDUCATION

The new emphasis on education during the Renaissance period benefited the women of wealthy families, who were often tutored in their own homes. The advent of printing made books much more widely available, and that enabled educated women to pursue interests such as medicine, religion, and the classics. Educated women did not expect to have a career, but might become ladies of the court, ornaments of aristocratic households, or patrons of the arts. One influential Renaissance patron was Marguerite of Navarre (1492–1549), the sister of the French king Francis I. Marguerite's court was a center of humanist learning and religious tolerance. She was also a gifted writer. Another noblewoman who received a humanist education, Sofonisba Anguissola (about 1532–1625), became the first important woman artist of the Renaissance.

As the number of highly educated women increased, so did the number of women who became writers. In particular there were many important women poets, such as the Italian Vittoria Colonna (1492–1547), who

---

The Renaissance emphasis on education benefited women of wealthy families

---

wrote love sonnets and was a close friend of Michelangelo. They wrote letters and sonnets to each other, and Michelangelo painted at least three works for her. The French poet Louise Labé urged her fellow women to express themselves through the written word for their own pleasure.

Social custom restricted the number of topics that women could write about. They were expected to confine

Right: A 16th-century painting of a woman shortly after giving birth. Childbirth was risky during the Renaissance period, and many women—both rich and poor—died giving birth.

themselves to writing on love or religious subjects—hymns, poems, devotional works, and translations. Humanist teaching had opened their minds, but society restricted their potential. Christine de Pisan, the poet, essayist, and historian who was very unusual in that she supported her family by her writing, lamented that she had not been "born into this world as a member of the masculine sex."

WOMEN RULERS

A few women attained unusual political prominence as queens or powerful regents during the Renaissance. Most of them were highly educated, trained in Latin, modern languages, and the fine arts. Isabella of Castille (ruled 1474–1504) was a powerful and devout monarch, who with her husband and coruler, Ferdinand, united Spain, expelled the last of the Muslim Moors from the southern kingdom of Granada, sponsored Christopher Columbus on his epoch-making journey to the New World, and created a brilliant court, peopled by scholars, artists, and prominent churchmen.

In the 16th century England was ruled by two successive queens who both left a strong imprint. Mary Tudor (ruled 1553–1558) was a devoted Catholic who dedicated herself to restoring Protestant England to what she believed to be the "true" faith of Catholicism. She was disliked and feared because of her marriage to Philip II of Spain and her harsh

Left: A 15th-century painting by Francesco Botticini (1446–1497) showing Saint Monica founding the order of the Augustinian nuns. Joining a religious order was often a woman's only alternative to marriage.

BLOODY MARY

The Catholic English queen Mary I (ruled 1553–1558) was known as "Bloody Mary" because of her harsh treatment of her Protestant subjects. The daughter of Henry VIII and his first wife, Catherine of Aragon, Mary was born in 1516. After her father divorced her mother, she was declared illegitimate and grew up in constant fear of execution. In 1547 her younger brother succeeded his father as Edward VI and introduced many Protestant reforms.

After Edward's death in 1553 Mary became queen. She was determined to return England to the Catholic faith—by force if necessary. Against the wishes of her advisers, she decided to marry the leading champion of the Catholic church, Philip II of Spain. In February 1554 a Protestant rebellion led by Sir Thomas Wyatt broke out in protest at the marriage. The rebellion was put down, and Wyatt and a hundred other rebels were executed for treason. Mary's Spanish marriage went ahead. In 1555 Mary's persecution of Protestants began. Her informers and spies generated an atmosphere of fear and suspicion throughout the country. In three years a total of 237 men and 52 women were burned at the stake as heretics. Mary was hated and feared by her subjects, who were further alienated by an unsuccessful war with France. In addition Mary's marriage proved unhappy and childless. She died on November 17, 1558, and her attempts to restore the Catholic faith died with her.

Above: A 16th-century portrait of Mary I, queen of England. During her short reign Mary instigated a reign of terror against her Protestant subjects.

treatment of Protestants. She was succeeded by her half-sister Elizabeth I (ruled 1558–1603), whose reign, by contrast, the English saw as a golden age. Elizabeth supported a tolerant form of Protestantism, kept the Spanish at bay, and presided over a brilliant court exemplified by the works of William Shakespeare and Edmund Spenser. Elsewhere in Europe women achieved prominence as regents. Margaret of Parma ruled the Netherlands from 1559 to 1567, and Catherine de Medici effectively ruled France for nearly 30 years as regent for her three young sons.

Rule by women was frequently resented. In 1558 John Knox, the architect of the Scottish Reformation, wrote *The First Blast of the Trumpet against the Monstrous Regiment of Women*, which argued that female rule was contrary to divine and natural law. In the Renaissance it was generally believed that women were inferior both intellectually and physically to men. In fact, women proved themselves to be neither better nor worse than men as rulers. Their success or lack of it depended on their strength of character and the set of circumstances in which they found themselves.

SEE ALSO

- Anguissola
- Borgia Family
- Capitalism
- Christine de Pisan
- Daily Life
- Education
- Elizabeth I
- Families
- Gentileschi
- Joan of Arc
- Marguerite of Navarre
- Religious Orders

Zoology

Above: A woodcut of a rhinoceros made in 1515 by Albrecht Dürer. The woodcut is based on careful research and close observation of nature.

Zoology is the branch of biology that studies animals. During the Renaissance European explorers discovered many new animals, creating an upsurge of interest in the animal kingdom.

In the 15th and early 16th centuries zoology was dominated by legends and folklore. Much information about animals still came from ancient texts, such as the 37-volume encyclopedia by the Roman writer Pliny (about 61–112 A.D.). These books included mythical animals like the unicorn, sphinx, and sea monsters. Their authors often did not make a distinction between real and fictional creatures. Even the illustrations of real animals were sometimes highly inaccurate, because the artists had never seen them.

EXOTIC WILDLIFE

Two factors helped modern zoology develop during the Renaissance. The invention of the printing press in the 1450s meant that information was much more easily available and more accurate. And there was great interest in the wildlife found by the explorers of the Americas, Africa, and Asia. Many books and pamphlets were written to meet this demand.

Artists began to make more accurate images of animals based on careful observation and research. The most famous of them include a woodcut of a rhinoceros made by Albrecht Dürer (1471–1528) in 1515 and numerous pen drawings of horses, insects, and other species (categories of mammals, birds, fish, and insects) by Leonardo da Vinci (1452–1519).

In 1551 the Swiss physician Konrad Gesner (1516–1565) published a revolutionary book called *Historia animalium* ("The History of Animals"), in which he tried to describe every known animal. Gesner included many recently discovered animals, such as American bison, sloths, toucans, and

COSIMO'S ZOO

Some of the richest rulers and nobles of the Renaissance period kept their own private zoos. One of the most famous of these zoos belonged to Cosimo de Medici (1389–1464) of Florence. Cosimo had long wanted a giraffe and finally received one from Africa. To find out whether the bizarre-looking animal was by nature more like a camel or a panther, he put the giraffe in a cage together with some lions, bulls, and hounds. The other animals ignored the terrified giraffe, which managed to survive this cruel experiment.

THE MEETING OF TWO NATURES

Besides discovering new species of animals in the Americas, the early European explorers also introduced to the "New World" animals that did not live there naturally. Columbus shipped over cows, oxen, pigs, and hens, none of which are native to the Americas. The Spanish conquistadores introduced horses to Mexico and South America. By the mid-16th century horses had reached North America too. In this way the European explorers actually changed the variety of wildlife found in the Americas.

SEE ALSO

♦ Books and Libraries
♦ Botany
♦ Drawing
♦ Dürer
♦ Exploration
♦ Leonardo da Vinci
♦ Printing

hummingbirds, as well as detailed descriptions of animals that Europeans had known about for centuries, such as camels and giraffes. For the first time Gesner illustrated aspects of animal behavior, such as a killer whale attacking a great whale.

LIFE BENEATH THE WAVES

Also in 1551 the French traveler Pierre Belon (1517–1564) published a guide to the wildlife of the seas. Among the hundreds of sea creatures that Belon described were swordfish, sea horses, flying fish, octopuses, sponges, and jellyfish. In 1555 Belon published a book about birds that included illustrations of bird and human skeletons side by side so that readers could compare them.

However, naturalists like Gesner and Belon still found it difficult to collect accurate information. They made many mistakes. Giant sea serpents and other imaginary beasts continued to appear in zoology textbooks until well into the 17th century. It was not until the 18th century that scientists made a serious effort to classify the animal kingdom.

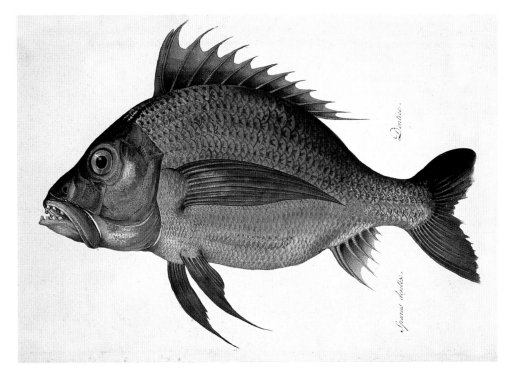

Left: An engraving of a sea bream by Jacopo Ligozzi (about 1547–1632). The maps and diaries of the early explorers of the Americas, Africa, and Asia often described lands of lush beauty, with rivers alive with jumping fish.

Zwingli

The Swiss preacher Huldrych Zwingli (1484–1531) was one of the most important figures of the Reformation—the movement that resulted in the church being split between Catholics and Protestants. His preaching in the city of Zurich began the Reformation in Switzerland in the 1520s.

Born in Wildhaus in Switzerland in 1484, Zwingli was educated at Basel, Bern, and Vienna University. He was particularly influenced by the ideas of Erasmus, the great humanist thinker and scholar. As a result, Zwingli studied the writings of the early church fathers and the New Testament in Greek. He became a priest in 1506. Seven years later he accompanied Swiss mercenary soldiers to Italy as their chaplain, and his experiences led him to denounce

Zwingli preached that the Bible, not the church, was the most important authority in a Christian's life

the mercenary system. In 1516 he served as a priest at Einsiedeln, where he began to gather his thoughts about his understanding of the scriptures and the need for church reform.

In 1518 Zwingli moved to Zurich, where he was elected "people's preacher" at the cathedral. On New Year's Day 1519 he began to preach a series of sermons on the New

Testament. Zwingli preached that the Bible, not the church, was the most important authority in a Christian's life. People should do only what the Bible commanded and refrain from anything that did not have biblical authority. By 1522 the people of Zurich, who had eagerly responded to his teachings, were ready to embrace the Protestant revolution that had begun a few years earlier in Germany. In 1523 Zurich became the first Protestant state outside Germany.

REJECTING THE POPE
Like the German reformer Martin Luther, Zwingli rejected the authority of the pope, and he believed that priests should be allowed to marry. But his position was more extreme than that of Luther, who did allow some traditional

Above: A 16th-century painting of Zwingli. The Swiss Reformation that he initiated in Zurich was achieved smoothly without opposition. After the city had rejected the authority of the Catholic bishop of Constance, the city council took charge of religious affairs.

church practices. Zwingli, for example, told the people of Zurich that they should sing in church without an organ accompaniment and should take down crosses and holy images (paintings and statues) from the walls, insisting there was no support for them in the Bible.

BODY AND BLOOD

Zwingli also disagreed dramatically with the church about the significance of the Mass, or Eucharist—the ritual celebration of Christ's Last Supper with his disciples. The Catholic church taught that during the Mass the offerings of bread and wine when consecrated (made holy by the priest's words) became in substance the body and blood of Christ. Zwingli strongly disagreed. He believed that the bread and wine were only symbols of Christ's body and blood and nothing more. For him the most important part of a church service was the sermon. Zwingli's disagreement with Luther

about points of practice and doctrine (teachings) threatened to split the Protestants, who needed to stand united against the powerful Catholic church. So in 1529 the German Protestant noble Philip of Hesse invited Zwingli and Luther to his castle at Marburg to settle their differences. Although they reached agreement on many points of doctrine, they were unable to reach complete agreement.

SWISS REFORMATION

Meanwhile, Zwingli's ideas had been adopted by the Swiss cantons, or districts, of Bern, Basel, Schaffhausen, Glarus, and Saint Gall. But other districts, known as the "forest cantons," including Lucerne and Zug, remained loyal to the Catholic church. Friction between the two sides grew and in 1529 nearly exploded into all-out war. Two years later fighting between the two sides did break out, and Zwingli was killed on the field of battle.

SEE ALSO
- Biblical Studies
- Calvin
- Luther
- Protestantism
- Reformation

Left: A 16th-century engraving of the meeting between Zwingli and the German reformer Martin Luther (both standing, right) at Marburg, Germany, in 1529. Although they were able to agree on many points of doctrine, they were unable to resolve all their differences, so their two brands of Protestantism remained separate.

Timeline

♦ **1305** Giotto begins work on frescoes for the Arena Chapel, Padua—he is often considered the father of Renaissance art.

♦ **1321** Dante publishes the *Divine Comedy*, which has a great influence on later writers.

♦ **1327** Petrarch begins writing the sonnets known as the *Canzoniere*.

♦ **1337** The start of the Hundred Years' War between England and France.

♦ **1353** Boccaccio writes the *Decameron*, an influential collection of 100 short stories.

♦ **1368** The Ming dynasty comes to power in China.

♦ **1377** Pope Gregory XI moves the papacy back to Rome from Avignon, where it has been based since 1309.

♦ **1378** The Great Schism begins: two popes, Urban VI and Clement VII, both lay claim to the papacy.

♦ **1378** English theologian John Wycliffe criticizes the practices of the Roman Catholic church.

♦ **1380** Ivan I of Muscovy defeats the army of the Mongol Golden Horde at the battle of Kulikovo.

♦ **1389** The Ottomans defeat the Serbs at the battle of Kosovo, beginning a new phase of Ottoman expansion.

♦ **1397** Sigismund of Hungary is defeated by the Ottoman Turks at the battle of Nicopolis.

♦ **1397** Queen Margaret of Denmark unites Denmark, Sweden, and Norway under the Union of Kalmar.

♦ **1398** The Mongol leader Tamerlane invades India.

♦ **1399** Henry Bolingbroke becomes Henry IV of England.

♦ **1400** English writer Geoffrey Chaucer dies, leaving his *Canterbury Tales* unfinished.

♦ **1403** In Italy the sculptor Ghiberti wins a competition to design a new set of bronze doors for Florence Cathedral.

♦ **c.1402** The Bohemian preacher Jan Hus begins to attack the corruption of the church.

♦ **1405** The Chinese admiral Cheng Ho commands the first of seven expeditions to the Indian Ocean and East Africa.

♦ **1415** Jan Hus is summoned to the Council of Constance and condemned to death.

♦ **1415** Henry V leads the English to victory against the French at the battle of Agincourt.

♦ **c.1415** Florentine sculptor Donatello produces his sculpture *Saint George*.

♦ **1416** Venice defeats the Ottoman fleet at the battle of Gallipoli, but does not check the Ottoman advance.

♦ **1417** The Council of Constance elects Martin V pope, ending the Great Schism.

♦ **1418** Brunelleschi designs the dome of Florence Cathedral.

♦ **1420** Pope Martin V returns the papacy to Rome, bringing peace and order to the city.

♦ **c.1420** Prince Henry of Portugal founds a school of navigation at Sagres, beginning a great age of Portuguese exploration.

♦ **1422** Charles VI of France dies, leaving his throne to the English king Henry VI. Charles VI's son also claims the throne.

♦ **c.1425** Florentine artist Masaccio paints the *Holy Trinity*, the first painting to use the new science of perspective.

♦ **1429** Joan of Arc leads the French to victory at Orléans; Charles VII is crowned king of France in Reims Cathedral.

♦ **1431** The English burn Joan of Arc at the stake for heresy.

♦ **1433** Sigismund of Luxembourg becomes Holy Roman emperor.

♦ **1434** Cosimo de Medici comes to power in Florence.

♦ **1434** The Flemish artist Jan van Eyck paints the *Arnolfini Marriage* using the newly developed medium of oil paint.

♦ **1439** The Council of Florence proclaims the reunion of the Western and Orthodox churches.

♦ **c.1440** Donatello completes his statue of David—the first life-size bronze sculpture since antiquity.

♦ **1443** Federigo da Montefeltro becomes ruler of Urbino.

♦ **1447** The Milanese people declare their city a republic.

♦ **1450** The condottiere Francesco Sforza seizes control of Milan.

♦ **1450** Fra Angelico paints *The Annunciation* for the monastery of San Marco in Florence.

♦ **1453** Constantinople, capital of the Byzantine Empire, falls to the Ottomans and becomes the capital of the Muslim Empire.

♦ **1453** The French defeat the English at the battle of Castillon, ending the Hundred Years' War.

♦ **1454–1456** Venice, Milan, Florence, Naples, and the papacy form the Italian League to maintain peace in Italy.

♦ **1455** The start of the Wars of the Roses between the Houses of York and Lancaster in England.

♦ **c.1455** The German Johannes Gutenberg develops the first printing press using movable type.

♦ **1456** The Florentine painter Uccello begins work on the *Battle of San Romano*.

♦ **1461** The House of York wins the Wars of the Roses; Edward IV becomes king of England.

♦ **1461** Sonni Ali becomes king of the Songhai Empire in Africa.

♦ **1462** Marsilio Ficino founds the Platonic Academy of Florence— the birthplace of Renaissance Neoplatonism.

♦ **1463** War breaks out between Venice and the Ottoman Empire.

♦ **1465** The Italian painter Mantegna begins work on the Camera degli Sposi in Mantua.

♦ **1467** Civil war breaks out in Japan, lasting for over a century.

♦ **1469** Lorenzo the Magnificent, grandson of Cosimo de Medici, comes to power in Florence.

♦ **1469** The marriage of Isabella I of Castile and Ferdinand V of Aragon unites the two kingdoms.

♦ **1470** The Florentine sculptor Verrocchio completes his *David*.

♦ **1476** William Caxton establishes the first English printing press at Westminster, near London.

♦ **1477** Pope Sixtus IV begins building the Sistine Chapel.

♦ **c.1477** Florentine painter Sandro Botticelli paints the *Primavera*, one of the first large-scale mythological paintings of the Renaissance.

♦ **1478** The Spanish Inquisition is founded in Spain.

♦ **1480** The Ottoman fleet destroys the port of Otranto in south Italy.

♦ **1485** Henry Tudor becomes Henry VII of England—the start of the Tudor dynasty.

♦ **1486** *The Witches' Hammer* is published, a handbook on how to hunt down witches.

♦ **1488** Portuguese navigator Bartholomeu Dias reaches the Cape of Good Hope.

♦ **1491** Missionaries convert King Nzina Nkowu of the Congo to Christianity.

♦ **1492** The Spanish monarchs conquer Granada, the last Moorish territory in Spain.

♦ **1492** Christopher Columbus lands in the Bahamas, claiming the territory for Spain.

♦ **1492** Henry VII of England renounces all English claims to the French throne.

♦ **1493** The Hapsburg Maximilian becomes Holy Roman emperor.

♦ **1494** Charles VIII of France invades Italy, beginning four decades of Italian wars.

♦ **1494** In Italy Savonarola comes to power in Florence.

♦ **1494** The Treaty of Tordesillas divides the non-Christian world between Spain and Portugal.

♦ **1495** Leonardo da Vinci begins work on *The Last Supper* .

♦ **1495** Spain forms a Holy League with the Holy Roman emperor and expels the French from Naples.

♦ **1498** Portuguese navigator Vasco da Gama reaches Calicut, India.

♦ **1498** German artist Dürer creates the *Apocalypse* woodcuts.

♦ **1500** Portuguese navigator Pedro Cabral discovers Brazil.

♦ **c.1500–1510** Dutch painter Hieronymus Bosch paints *The Garden of Earthly Delights*.

♦ **c.1502** Italian architect Donato Bramante designs the Tempietto Church in Rome.

♦ **1503** Leonardo da Vinci begins painting the *Mona Lisa*.

♦ **1504** Michelangelo finishes his statue of David, widely seen as a symbol of Florence.

♦ **c.1505** Venetian artist Giorgione paints *The Tempest*.

♦ **1506** The Italian architect Donato Bramante begins work on rebuilding Saint Peter's, Rome.

♦ **1508** Michelangelo begins work on the ceiling of the Sistine Chapel in the Vatican.

♦ **1509** Henry VIII ascends the throne of England.

♦ **1509** The League of Cambrai defeats Venice at the battle of Agnadello.

♦ **1510–1511** Raphael paints *The School of Athens* in the Vatican.

♦ **1511** The French are defeated at the battle of Ravenna in Italy and are forced to retreat over the Alps.

♦ **1513** Giovanni de Medici becomes Pope Leo X.

♦ **1515** Thomas Wolsey becomes lord chancellor of England.

♦ **1515** Francis I becomes king of France. He invades Italy and captures Milan.

♦ **c.1515** German artist Grünewald paints the *Isenheim Altarpiece.*

♦ **1516** Charles, grandson of the emperor Maximilian I, inherits the Spanish throne as Charles I.

♦ **1516** Thomas More publishes his political satire *Utopia.*

♦ **1516** Dutch humanist Erasmus publishes a more accurate version of the Greek New Testament.

♦ **1517** Martin Luther pins his 95 theses on the door of the castle church in Wittenburg.

♦ **1519** Charles I of Spain becomes Holy Roman emperor Charles V.

♦ **1519–1521** Hernán Cortés conquers Mexico for Spain.

♦ **1520** Henry VIII of England and Francis I of France meet at the Field of the Cloth of Gold to sign a treaty of friendship.

♦ **1520** Portuguese navigator Ferdinand Magellan discovers a route to the Indies around the tip of South America.

♦ **1520** Süleyman the Magnificent becomes ruler of the Ottoman Empire, which now dominates the eastern Mediterranean.

♦ **1520–1523** Titian paints *Bacchus and Ariadne* for Alfonso d'Este.

♦ **1521** Pope Leo X excommuicates Martin Luther.

♦ **1521** The emperor Charles V attacks France, beginning a long period of European war.

♦ **1522** Ferdinand Magellan's ship the *Victoria* is the first to sail around the world.

♦ **1523–1525** Huldrych Zwingli sets up a Protestant church at Zurich in Switzerland.

♦ **1525** In Germany the Peasants' Revolt is crushed, and its leader, Thomas Münzer, is executed.

♦ **1525** The emperor Charles V defeats the French at the battle of Pavia and takes Francis I prisoner.

♦ **1525** William Tyndale translates the New Testament into English.

♦ **1526** The Ottoman Süleyman the Magnificent defeats Hungary at the battle of Mohács.

♦ **1526** Muslim Mongol leader Babur invades northern India and establishes the Mogul Empire.

♦ **c.1526** The Italian artist Correggio paints the *Assumption of the Virgin* in Parma Cathedral.

♦ **1527** Charles V's armies overrun Italy and sack Rome.

♦ **1527–1530** Gustavus I founds a Lutheran state church in Sweden.

♦ **1528** Italian poet and humanist Baldassare Castiglione publishes *The Courtier.*

♦ **1529** The Ottoman Süleyman the Magnificent lays siege to Vienna, but eventually retreats.

♦ **1530** The Catholic church issues the "Confutation," attacking Luther and Protestantism.

♦ **1531** The Protestant princes of Germany form the Schmalkaldic League.

♦ **1531–1532** Francisco Pizarro conquers Peru for Spain.

♦ **1532** Machiavelli's *The Prince* is published after his death.

♦ **1533** Henry VIII of England rejects the authority of the pope and marries Anne Boleyn.

♦ **1533** Anabaptists take over the city of Münster in Germany.

♦ **1533** Christian III of Denmark founds the Lutheran church of Denmark.

♦ **1534** Paul III becomes pope and encourages the growth of new religious orders such as the Jesuits.

♦ **1534** Luther publishes his German translation of the Bible.

♦ **1534** The Act of Supremacy declares Henry VIII supreme head of the Church of England.

♦ **c.1535** Parmigianino paints the mannerist masterpiece *Madonna of the Long Neck.*

♦ **1535–1536** The Swiss city of Geneva becomes Protestant and expels the Catholic clergy.

♦ **1536** Calvin publishes *Institutes of the Christian Religion*, which sets out his idea of predestination.

♦ **1536** Pope Paul III sets up a reform commission to examine the state of the Catholic church.

♦ **1537** Hans Holbein is appointed court painter to Henry VIII of England.

♦ **1539** Italian painter Bronzino begins working for Cosimo de Medici the Younger in Florence.

♦ **1539** Ignatius de Loyola founds the Society of Jesus (the Jesuits).

♦ **1541** John Calvin sets up a model Christian city in Geneva.

♦ **1543** Andreas Vesalius publishes *On the Structure of the Human Body*, a handbook of anatomy based on dissections.

♦ **1543** Polish astronomer Copernicus's *On the Revolutions of the Heavenly Spheres* proposes a sun-centered universe.

♦ **1544** Charles V and Francis I of France sign the Truce of Crespy.

♦ **1545** Pope Paul III organizes the Council of Trent to counter the threat of Protestantism.

♦ **1545** Spanish explorers find huge deposits of silver in the Andes Mountains of Peru.

♦ **1547** Charles V defeats the Protestant Schmalkaldic League at the Battle of Mühlberg.

♦ **1547** Ivan IV "the Terrible" declares himself czar of Russia.

♦ **1548** Titian paints the equestrian portrait *Charles V after the Battle of Mühlberg.*

♦ **1548** Tintoretto paints *Saint Mark Rescuing the Slave.*

♦ **1550** Italian Georgio Vasari publishes his *Lives of the Artists.*

♦ **1553** Mary I of England restores the Catholic church.

♦ **1554** Work begins on the Cathedral of Saint Basil in Red Square, Moscow.

♦ **1555** At the Peace of Augsburg Charles V allows the German princes to determine their subjects' religion.

♦ **1556** Ivan IV defeats the last Mongol khanates. Muscovy now dominates the Volga region.

♦ **1556** Philip II becomes king of Spain.

♦ **1559** Elizabeth I of England restores the Protestant church.

♦ **1562** The Wars of Religion break out in France.

♦ **1565** Flemish artist Pieter Bruegel the Elder paints *Hunters in the Snow.*

♦ **1565** Italian architect Palladio designs the Villa Rotunda, near Vicenza.

♦ **1566** The Dutch revolt against the Spanish over the loss of political and religious freedoms:

Philip II of Spain sends 10,000 troops under the duke of Alba to suppress the revolt.

♦ **1569** Flemish cartographer Mercator produces a world map using a new projection.

♦ **1571** Philip II of Spain and an allied European force defeat the Ottomans at the battle of Lepanto.

♦ **1572** In Paris, France, a Catholic mob murders thousands of Huguenots in the Saint Bartholomew's Day Massacre.

♦ **1572** Danish astronomer Tycho Brahe sees a new star.

♦ **1573** Venetian artist Veronese paints the *Feast of the House of Levi.*

♦ **1579** The seven northern provinces of the Netherlands form the Union of Utrecht.

♦ **1580** Giambologna creates his mannerist masterpiece *Flying Mercury.*

♦ **1585** Henry III of France bans Protestantism in France; civil war breaks out again in the War of the Three Henrys.

♦ **1586** El Greco, a Greek artist active in Spain, paints the *Burial of Count Orgaz.*

♦ **1587** Mary, Queen of Scots, is executed by Elizabeth I of England.

♦ **c.1587** Nicholas Hilliard paints the miniature *Young Man among Roses.*

♦ **1588** Philip II of Spain launches his great Armada against England —but the fleet is destroyed.

♦ **1589** Henry of Navarre becomes king of France as Henry IV.

♦ **1592–1594** Tintoretto paints *The Last Supper.*

♦ **1596** Edmund Spencer publishes the *Faerie Queene*, glorifying Elizabeth I as "Gloriana."

♦ **1598** Henry IV of France grants Huguenots and Catholics equal political rights.

♦ **1598** In England the Globe Theater is built on London's south bank; it stages many of Shakespeare's plays.

♦ **1600–1601** Caravaggio paints *The Crucifixion of Saint Peter*, an early masterpiece of baroque art.

♦ **1603** Elizabeth I of England dies and is succeeded by James I, son of Mary, Queen of Scots.

♦ **1610** Galileo's *The Starry Messenger* supports the sun-centered model of the universe.

♦ **1620** The Italian painter Artemisia Gentileschi paints *Judith and Holofernes.*

Glossary

A.D. The letters A.D. stand for the Latin Anno Domini, which means "in the year of our Lord." Dates with these letters written after them are measured forward from the year Christ was born.

Altarpiece A painting or sculpture placed behind an altar in a church.

Apprentice Someone (usually a young person) legally bound to a craftsman for a number of years in order to learn a craft.

Baptistery Part of a church, or a separate building, where people are baptized.

B.C. Short for "Before Christ." Dates with these letters after them are measured backward from the year of Christ's birth.

Bureaucracy A system of government that relies on a body of officials and usually involves much paperwork and many regulations.

Cameo A precious stone carved with a design that stands out from the background, often using the stone's different colors to enhance the effect.

Cardinal An official of the Catholic church, highest in rank below the pope. The cardinals elect the pope.

Classical A term used to describe the civilizations of ancient Greece and Rome. It is also used to describe any later art and architecture that is based on ancient Greek and Roman examples.

Commission An order for a specially made object, like a painting or tapestry.

Contemporary Someone or something that exists at the same period of time.

Curfew A regulation banning people from the streets, usually after dark.

Doctrine A specific principle or belief, or a system of beliefs, taught by the church.

Donor A person who gives or donates something. In the Renaissance people who paid for pictures with religious subjects often had their portraits included in them; this type of portrait is called a "donor portrait."

Economy The financial affairs of a country.

Equestrian A term used to describe something relating to a person on horseback. For example, an equestrian sculpture portrays a soldier or leader on horseback.

Foreshortening A technique used by artists in their pictures to recreate the appearance of objects when seen from a particular angle. It involves shortening some measurements, according to the laws of perspective (see below), to make it look as if objects are projecting toward or receding away from the surface of the picture.

Fresco A type of painting usually used for decorating walls and ceilings in which pigments (colors) are painted into wet plaster.

Guild An association of merchants or craftsmen organized to protect the interests of its members and to regulate the quality of their goods and services.

Heretic Someone whose beliefs contradict those of the church.

Humanism A new way of thinking about human life that characterized the Renaissance. It was based on study of the "humanities"— that is, ancient Greek and Roman texts, history, and philosophy—and stressed the importance of developing rounded, cultured people.

Laity or lay people Anyone who is not of the clergy.

Mercenary A soldier who will fight for any employer in return for money.

Moat A wide, water-filled ditch that is dug around a fortified building or town for defensive purposes.

Monopoly Exclusive rights or control over something.

Mosaic A picture or surface decoration made up of lots of small pieces of a material in different colors.

Patron Someone who orders and pays for a work of art.

Patronage The act of ordering and paying for a work of art.

Perspective A technique that allows artists to create the impression of three-dimensional space in their pictures. Near objects are made to appear larger, and distant objects are shown as smaller.

Satire A piece of writing that holds up human vices or follies to ridicule or scorn.

Scuola A type of charitable organization in Venice run under the guidance of the church and devoted to good works. Each *scuola* was financed by subscriptions from its members and often spent lavishly on ordering new architecture, sculpture, and paintings.

Siege A military blockade of a castle or town to force it to surrender, often by cutting off its supplies of food and water.

Species A term used in the classification of the natural world to describe a group of plants or animals that share common characteristics.

Tempera A type of paint made by mixing pigments (colors) with egg yolk. It was widely used in the Middle Ages and Renaissance.

Theologian Someone who makes a study of religion.

Treatise A book or long essay about the principles, or rules, of a particular subject.

Triumphal arch A huge, freestanding arch decorated with sculpture built by the ancient Romans to celebrate a great military victory or leader. Processions passed through the arch as part of victory celebrations.

Vassal A person who is bound to a local lord to whom they owe their loyalty and services.

Vendetta A sustained campaign of hate and violence against someone.

Vernacular The language of the ordinary people of a country, rather than a literary or formal language like Latin.

Further Reading

Arnold, Thomas F. *The Renaissance at War*. London: Cassell, 2001.

Biadene, Susanna. *Titian: Prince of Painters*. New York: Prestel USA, 1990.

Borsi, Franco, and Stefano Borsi. *Paolo Uccello*. New York: Harry N. Abrams, 1994.

Bremer-David, Charissa. *French Tapestries and Textiles in the J. Paul Getty Museum*. Los Angeles, CA: J. Paul Getty Museum Publications, 1997.

Brewer, Paul. *Warfare in the Renaissance World*. Austin, TX: Raintree/Steck Vaughn, 1998.

Brockman, John. *The Greatest Inventions of the Past 2,000 Years*. New York: Simon & Schuster, 2000.

Brown, Patricia Fortini. *Art and Life in Renaissance Venice*. New York: Harry N. Abrams, 1997.

Bruschini, Enrico. *In the Footsteps of Popes: A Spirited Guide to the Treasures of the Vatican*. New York: William Morrow, 2001.

Butterfield, Andrew. *The Sculptures of Andrea Del Verrocchio*. New Haven, CT: Yale University Press, 1997.

Casson, Hugh Maxwell. *Hugh Casson's Oxford*. London: Phaidon Press, 1998.

Clough, Cecil H. *The Duchy of Urbino in the Renaissance*. London: Variorum Reprints, 1981.

Day, Nancy. *Your Travel Guide to Renaissance Europe*. Minneapolis, MN: Runestone Press, 2001.

Diefendorf, Barbara B. *Beneath the Cross: Catholics and Huguenots in Sixteenth-Century Paris*. Oxford: Oxford University Press, 1991.

Erlanger, Philippe. *St. Bartholomew's Night*. Westport, CT: Greenwood Press, 1975.

Gallagher, Jim. *Vasco da Gama and the Portuguese Explorer*. Broomall, PA: Chelsea House Publishers, 2000.

Geijer, Agnes. *A History of Textile Art*. New York: Rizzoli, 1982.

Gesner, Konrad. *Beasts and Animals in Decorative Woodcuts of the Renaissance*. New York: Dover Publications, 1983.

Gilbert, Creighton. *Michelangelo: On and Off the Sistine Ceiling*. New York: George Braziller, 1994.

Giudici, Vittorio. *The Sistine Chapel: Its History and Masterpieces*. New York: Peter Bedrick Books, 2000.

Goldthwaite, Richard A. *Wealth and the Demand for Art in Italy, 1300–1600*. Baltimore, MD: Johns Hopkins University Press, 1993.

Goodman, Joan Elizabeth. *A Long and Uncertain Journey: The 27,000 Mile Voyage of Vasco da Gama*. New York: Mikaya Press, 2001.

Goss, John. *The City Maps of Europe: 16th Century Town Plans from Braun and Hogenberg*. Chicago, IL: Rand McNally, 1992.

Grendler, Paul F. *The Universities of the Italian Renaissance*. Baltimore, MD: Johns Hopkins University Press, 2002.

Hale, J.R. *Artists and Warfare in the Renaissance*. New Haven, CT: Yale University Press, 1991.

Hall, Bert S. *Weapons and Warfare in Renaissance Europe: Gunpowder, Technology, and Tactics*. Baltimore: Johns Hopkins University Press, 1997.

Harris, Jennifer. *Textiles 5,000 Years: An International History and Illustrated Survey*. New York: Harry N. Abrams, 1993.

Headley, John M. *Tommaso Campanella and the Transformation of the World*. Princeton, NJ: Princeton University Press, 1997.

Hopkins, Andrea. *Most Wise and Valiant Ladies*. London: Collins & Brown, 1997.

Howard, Deborah. *Jacopo Sansovino: Architecture and Patronage in Renaissance Venice*. New Haven, CT: Yale University Press, 1987.

Kirby, David, and Merja-Liisa Hinkkanen. *The Baltic and the North Seas*. London: Routledge, 2000.

Lane, Frederic Chapin. *Venetian Ships and Shipbuilders of the Renaissance*. Baltimore, MD: Johns Hopkins University Press, 1992.

León, Vicki. *Outrageous Women of the Renaissance*. New York: John Wiley, 1999.

León, Vicki. *Uppity Women of the Renaissance*. Berkeley, CA: Conari Press, 1999.

Meyer, Carolyn. *Mary, Bloody Mary*. San Diego, CA: Harcourt Brace, 1999.

More, Thomas, Henry Neville, and Francis Bacon. *Three Early Modern Utopias: Utopia, New Atlantis, The Isle of Pines*. Oxford: Oxford University Press, 1999.

North, Michael. *Art and Commerce in the Dutch Golden Age*. New Haven: Yale University Press, 1999.

Norwich, John Julius. *A History of Venice*. New York: Vintage Books, 1989.

Paolieri, Annarita. *Paolo Uccello, Domenico Veneziano, Andrea del Castagno*. New York: Riverside Book Company, 1991.

Pedrocco, Filippo. *Titian*. New York: Rizzoli, 2001.

Pernis, Maria Grazia. *Federico da Montefeltro and Sigismondo Malatesta: The Eagle and the Elephant*. New York: Peter Lang, 1996.

Priver, Andreas. *Veronese*. Cologne, Germany: Könemann, 2001.

Satkowski, Leon. *Giorgio Vasari*. Princeton, NJ: Princeton University Press, 1994.

Usher, Abbot Payson. *A History of Mechanical Inventions*. New York: Dover Publications, 1988.

Williams, Trevor. *A History of Invention: From Stone Axes to Silicon Chips*. New York: Checkmark Books, 2000.

Zuffi, Stefano. *Art in Venice*. New York: Harry N. Abrams, 1999.

WEBSITES

World history site
www.historyworld.net

BBC Online: History
www.bbc.co.uk/history

The Webmuseum's tour of the Renaissance
www.oir.ucf.edu/wm/paint/glo/renaissance/

Virtual time travel tour of the Renaissance
library.thinkquest.org/3588/Renaissance/

The Renaissance
www.learner.org/exhibits/renaissance

National Gallery of Art—tour of 16th-century Italian paintings
www.nga.gov/collection/gallery/ita16.htm

Uffizi Art Gallery, Florence
musa.uffizi.firenze.it/welcomeE.html

Database of Renaissance artists
www.artcyclopedia.com/index.html

Set Index

MAPS
The maps in this book show the locations of cities, states, and empires of the
Renaissance period. However, for the sake of clarity, present-day place names are
often used.